A TOUR IN IRELAND. 1776-1779
BY
Arthur Young

A TOUR IN IRELAND. 1776-1779

Published by Wallachia Publishers

New York City, NY

First published circa 1820

ABOUT WALLACHIA PUBLISHERS

<u>Wallachia Publishers</u> mission is to publish the world's finest European history texts. More information on our recent publications and catalog can be found on our website.

A TOUR IN IRELAND. 1776-1779.

By
ARTHUR YOUNG.
CASSELL & COMPANY, Limited:
london, paris, new york & melbourne.
1897.

INTRODUCTION.

Arthur Young was born in 1741, the son of a clergyman, at Bradfield, in Suffolk. He was apprenticed to a merchant at Lynn, but his activity of mind caused him to be busy over many questions of the day. He wrote when he was seventeen a pamphlet on American politics, for which a publisher paid him with ten pounds' worth of books. He started a periodical, which ran to six numbers. He wrote novels. When he was twenty-eight years old his father died, and, being free to take his own course in life, he would have entered the army if his mother had not opposed. He settled down, therefore, to farming, and applied to farming all his zealous energy for reform, and all the labours of his busy pen. In 1768, a year before his father's death, he had published "A Six Weeks' Tour through the Southern Counties of England and Wales," which found many readers.

Between 1768 and 1771 Arthur Young produced also "The Farmer's Letters to the People of England, containing the Sentiments of a Practical Husbandman on the present State of Husbandry." In 1770 he published, in two thick quartos, "A Course of Experimental Agriculture, containing an exact Register of the Business transacted during Five Years on near 300 Acres of various Soils;" also in the same year appeared "Rural Economy; or, Essays on the Practical Part of Husbandry;" also in the same year "The Farmer's Guide in Hiring and Stocking Farms," in two volumes, with plans. Also in the same year appeared his "Farmer's Kalendar," of which the 215th edition was published in 1862. There had been a second edition of the "Six Weeks' Tour in the South of England," with enlargements, in 1769, and Arthur Young was encouraged to go on with increasing vigour to the publication of "The Farmer's Tour through the East of England: being a Register of a Journey through various Counties, to inquire into the State of Agriculture, Manufactures, and Population." This extended to four volumes, and appeared in the years 1770 and 1771. In 1771 also appeared, in four volumes, with plates, "A Six Months' Tour through the North of England, containing an Account of the Present State of Agriculture, Manufactures, and Population in several Counties of this Kingdom."

Thus Arthur Young took all his countrymen into counsel while he was learning his art, as a farmer who brought to his calling a vigorous spirit of inquiry with an activity in the diffusion of his thoughts that is a part of God's gift to the men who have thoughts to diffuse; the instinct for utterance being almost invariably joined to the power of suggesting what may help the world.

Whether he was essentially author turned farmer, or farmer turned author, Arthur Young has the first place in English literature as a farmer-author. Other practical men have written practical books of permanent value, which have places of honour in the literature of the farm; but Arthur Young's writings have won friends for themselves among readers of every class, and belong more broadly to the literature of the country.

Between 1766 and 1775 he says that he made £3,000 by his agricultural writings. The pen brought him more profit than the plough. He took a hundred acres in Hertfordshire, and said of them, "I know not what epithet to give this soil; sterility falls short of the idea; a hungry vitriolic gravel—I occupied for nine years the jaws of a wolf. A nabob's fortune would sink in the attempt to raise good arable crops in such a country. My experience and knowledge had increased from travelling and practice, but all was lost when exerted on such a spot." He tried at one time to balance his farm losses by reporting for the Morning Post, taking a seventeen-mile walk home to his farm every Saturday night.

In 1780 Arthur Young published this "Tour in Ireland, with General Observations on the Present State of that Kingdom in 1776-78." The general observations, which give to all his books a wide general interest, are, in this volume, of especial value to us now. It is here reprinted as given by Pinkerton.

In 1784 Arthur Young began to edit "Annals of Agriculture," which were continued through forty-five volumes. All writers in it were to sign their names, but when His Majesty King George III. contributed a description of Mr. Duckett's Farm at Petersham, he was allowed to sign himself "Ralph Robinson of Windsor."

In 1792 Arthur Young published the first quarto volume, and in 1794 the two volumes of his "Travels during the years 1787-8-9 and 1790, undertaken more particularly with a view of ascertaining the Cultivation, Wealth, Resources and National Prosperity of the Kingdom of France." This led to the official issue in France in 1801, by order of the Directory, of a translation of Young's agricultural works, under the title of "Le Cultivateur Anglais." Arthur Young also corresponded with Washington, and received recognition from the Empress Catherine of Russia, who sent him a gold snuff-box, and ermine cloaks for his wife and daughter. He was made a Fellow of the Royal Society.

In 1793 his labours led to the formation of a Board of Agriculture, of which he was appointed secretary.

When he was set at ease by this appointment, with a house and £400 a year, Arthur Young had been about to experiment on the reclaiming of four thousand acres of Yorkshire moorland. The Agricultural Board was dissolved in 1816, four years before surveys of the agriculture of each county were made for the Agricultural Board, Arthur Young himself contributing surveys of Hertfordshire, Lincolnshire, Oxfordshire, Norfolk, Suffolk, and Sussex.

Arthur Young's sight became dim in 1808, and blindness gradually followed. He died in 1820 at his native village of Bradfield, in Suffolk, at the age of seventy-nine years.

H. M.

A TOUR IN IRELAND.

June 19, 1776. Arrived at Holyhead, after an instructive journey through a part of England and Wales I had not seen before. Found the packet, the Claremont, Captain Taylor, would sail very soon. After a tedious passage of twenty-two hours, landed on the 20th in the morning, at Dunlary, four miles from Dublin, a city which much exceeded my expectation. The public buildings are magnificent, very many of the streets regularly laid out, and exceedingly well built. The front of the Parliament-house is grand, though not so light as a more open finishing of the roof would have made it. The apartments are spacious, elegant, and convenient, much beyond that heap of confusion at Westminster, so inferior to the magnificence to be looked for in the seat of empire. I was so fortunate as to arrive just in time to see Lord Harcourt, with the usual ceremonies, prorogue the Parliament. Trinity College is a beautiful building, and a numerous society; the library is a very fine room, and well filled. The new Exchange will be another edifice to do honour in Ireland; it is elegant, cost forty thousand pounds, but deserves a better situation. From everything I saw, I was struck with all those appearances of wealth which the capital of a thriving community may be supposed to exhibit. Happy if I find through the country in diffused prosperity the right source of this splendour! The common computation of inhabitants 200,000, but I should suppose exaggerated. Others guessed the number 140,000 or 150,000.

June 21. Introduced by Colonel Burton to the Lord Lieutenant, who was pleased to enter into conversation with me on my intended journey, made many remarks on the agriculture of several Irish counties, and showed himself to be an excellent farmer, particularly in draining. Viewed the Duke of Leinster's house, which is a very large stone edifice, the front simple but elegant, the pediment light; there are several good rooms; but a circumstance unrivalled is the court, which is spacious and magnificent, the opening behind the house is also beautiful. In the evening to the Rotunda, a circular room, ninety feet diameter, an imitation of Ranelagh, provided with a band of music.

The barracks are a vast building, raised in a plain style, of many divisions; the principal front is of an immense length. They contain every convenience for ten regiments.

June 23. Lord Charlemont's house in Dublin is equally elegant and convenient, the apartments large, handsome, and well disposed, containing some good pictures, particularly one by Rembrandt, of Judas throwing the money on the floor, with a strong expression of guilt and remorse; the whole group fine. In the same room is a portrait of Cæsar Borgia, by Titian. The library is a most elegant apartment of about forty by thirty, and of such a height as to form a pleasing proportion; the light is well managed, coming in from the cove of the ceiling, and has an exceeding good effect; at one end is a pretty ante-room, with a fine copy of the Venus de Medicis, and at the other two small rooms, one a cabinet of pictures and antiquities, the other medals. In the collection also of Robert Fitzgerald, Esq., in Merion Square, are several pieces which very well deserve a traveller's attention; it was the best I saw in Dublin. Before I quit that city I observe, on the houses in general, that what they call their two-roomed ones are good and

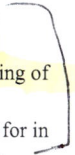

convenient. Mr. Latouche's, in Stephen's Green, I was shown as a model of this sort, and I found it well contrived, and finished elegantly. Drove to Lord Charlemont's villa at Marino, near the city, where his lordship has formed a pleasing lawn, margined in the higher part by a well-planted thriving shrubbery, and on a rising ground a banqueting-room, which ranks very high among the most beautiful edifices I have anywhere seen; it has much elegance, lightness, and effect, and commands a fine prospect. The rising ground on which it stands slopes off to an agreeable accompaniment of wood, beyond which on one side is Dublin Harbour, which here has the appearance of a noble river crowded with ships moving to and from the capital. On the other side is a shore spotted with white buildings, and beyond it the hills of Wicklow, presenting an outline extremely various. The other part of the view (it would be more perfect if the city was planted out) is varied, in some places nothing but wood, in others breaks of prospect. The lawn, which is extensive, is new grass, and appears to be excellently laid down, the herbage a fine crop of white clover (trifolium repens), trefoil, rib-grass (plantago lanceolata), and other good plants. Returned to Dublin, and made inquiries into other points, the prices of provisions, etc. The expenses of a family in proportion to those of London are, as five to eight.

Having the year following lived more than two months in Dublin, I am able to speak to a few points, which as a mere traveller I could not have done. The information I before received of the prices of living is correct. Fish and poultry are plentiful and very cheap. Good lodgings almost as dear as they are in London; though we were well accommodated (dirt excepted) for two guineas and a-half a week. All the lower ranks in this city have no idea of English cleanliness, either in apartments, persons, or cookery. There is a very good society in Dublin in a Parliament winter: a great round of dinners and parties; and balls and suppers every night in the week, some of which are very elegant; but you almost everywhere meet a company much too numerous for the size of the apartments. They have two assemblies on the plan of those of London, in Fishamble Street, and at the Rotunda; and two gentlemen's clubs, Anthry's and Daly's, very well regulated: I heard some anecdotes of deep play at the latter, though never to the excess common at London. An ill-judged and unsuccessful attempt was made to establish the Italian Opera, which existed but with scarcely any life for this one winter; of course they could rise no higher than a comic one. La Buona Figliuola, La Frascatana, and Il Geloso in Cimento, were repeatedly performed, or rather murdered, except the parts of Sestini. The house was generally empty, and miserably cold. So much knowledge of the state of a country is gained by hearing the debates of a Parliament, that I often frequented the gallery of the House of Commons. Since Mr. Flood has been silenced with the Vice-Treasurership of Ireland, Mr. Daly, Mr. Grattan, Sir William Osborn, and the prime serjeant Burgh, are reckoned high among the Irish orators. I heard many very eloquent speeches, but I cannot say they struck me like the exertion of the abilities of Irishmen in the English House of Commons, owing perhaps to the reflection both on the speaker and auditor, that the Attorney-General of England, with a dash of his pen, can reverse, alter, or entirely do away the matured result of all the eloquence, and all the abilities of this whole assembly. Before I conclude with Dublin I shall only remark, that walking in the streets there, from the narrowness and populousness of the principal thoroughfares, as well as from the dirt

2

and wretchedness of the canaille, is a most uneasy and disgusting exercise.

June 24. Left Dublin, and passed through the Phœnix Park, a very pleasing ground, at the bottom of which, to the left, the Liffey forms a variety of landscapes: this is the most beautiful environ of Dublin. Take the road to Luttrel's Town, through a various scenery on the banks of the river. That domain is a considerable one in extent, being above four hundred acres within the wall, Irish measure; in the front of the house is a fine lawn bounded by rich woods, through which are many ridings, four miles in extent. From the road towards the house they lead through a very fine glen, by the side of a stream falling over a rocky bed, through the dark woods, with great variety on the sides of steep slopes, at the bottom of which the Liffey is either heard or seen indistinctly. These woods are of great extent, and so near the capital, form a retirement exceedingly beautiful. Lord Irnham and Colonel Luttrel have brought in the assistance of agriculture to add to the beauties of the place; they have kept a part of the lands in cultivation in order to lay them down the better to grass; one hundred and fifty acres have been done, and above two hundred acres most effectually drained in the covered manner filled with stones. These works are well executed. The drains are also made under the roads in all wet places, with lateral short ones to take off the water instead of leaving it, as is common, to soak against the causeway, which is an excellent method. Great use has been made of limestone gravel in the improvements, the effect of which is so considerable, that in several spots where it was laid on ten years ago, the superiority of the grass is now similar to what one would expect from a fresh dunging.

Leaving Luttrel's Town I went to St. Wolstan's, which Lord Harcourt had been so obliging as to desire I would make my quarters, from whence to view to the right or left.

June 25. To Mr. Clement's, at Killadoon, who has lately built an excellent house, and planted much about it, with the satisfaction of finding that all his trees thrive well. I remarked the beech and larch seemed to get beyond the rest. He is also a good farmer.

June 26. Breakfasted with Colonel Marlay, at Cellbridge, found he had practised husbandry with much success, and given great attention to it from the peace of 1763, which put a period to a gallant scene of service in Germany. Walked through his grounds, which I found in general very well cultivated; his fences excellent; his ditches five by six and seven by six; the banks well made, and planted with quicks; the borders dug away, covered with lime till perfectly slacked, them mixed with dung and carried into the fields, a practice which Mr. Marlay has found of very great benefit.

Viewed Lucan, the seat of Agmondisham Vesey, Esq., on the banks of the Liffey. The house is rebuilding, but the wood on the river, with walks through it, is exceedingly beautiful. The character of the place is that of a sequestered shade. Distant views are everywhere shut out, and the objects all correspond perfectly with the impression they were designed to raise. It is a walk on the banks of the river, chiefly under a variety of fine wood, which rises on varied slopes, in some parts gentle, in others steep, spreading here and there into cool meadows, on the opposite shore, rich banks of wood or shrubby ground. The walk is perfectly sequestered, and has that melancholy gloom which should ever dwell in such a place. The river is of a character perfectly suited to the rest of the scenery, in some places breaking over rocks, in other silent, under the thick shade of spreading wood. Leaving Lucan, the next place is Leixlip, a fine one, on the river, with a fall, which in a wet season is considerable. Then St. Wolstan's, belonging to the Dean of Derry, a beautiful villa, which is also on the river; the grounds gay and open, though not without the advantage of much wood, disposed with judgment. A winding shrubbery quits the river, and is made to lead through some dressed ground that is pretty and cheerful.

Mr. Conolly's, at Castle Town, to which all travellers resort, is the finest house in Ireland, and not exceeded by many in England. It is a large handsome edifice, situated in the middle of an extensive lawn, which is quite surrounded with fine plantations disposed to the best advantage. To the north these unite into very large woods, through which many winding walks lead, with the convenience of several ornamented seats, rooms, etc. On the other side of the house, upon the river, is a cottage, with a shrubbery, prettily laid out; the house commands an extensive view, bounded by the Wicklow mountains. It consists of several noble apartments. On the first floor is a beautiful gallery, eighty feet long, elegantly fitted up.

June 27. Left Lord Harcourt's, and having received an invitation from the Duke of Leinster, passed through Mr. Conolly's grounds to his Grace's seat at Cartown. The park ranks among the finest in Ireland. It is a vast lawn, which waves over gentle hills, surrounded by plantations of great extent, and which break and divide in places so as to give much variety. A large but gentle vale winds through the whole, in the bottom of which a small stream has been enlarged into a fine river, which throws a cheerfulness through most of the scenes: over it a handsome stone bridge. There is a great variety on the banks of this vale; part of it consists of mild and gentle slopes, part steep banks of thick wood. In another place they are formed into a large shrubbery, very elegantly laid out, and dressed in the highest order, with a cottage, the scenery about which is uncommonly pleasing: and farther on this vale takes a stronger character, having a rocky bank on one side, and steep slopes scattered irregularly, with wood on the other. On one of the most rising grounds in the park is a tower, from the top of which the whole scenery is beheld; the park spreads on every side in fine sheets of lawn, kept in the highest order by eleven hundred sheep, scattered over with rich plantations, and bounded by a large margin of wood, through which is a riding.

From hence took the road to Summerhill, the seat of the Right Hon. H. L. Rowley. The country is cheerful and rich; and if the Irish cabins continue like what I have hitherto seen, I shall not hesitate to pronounce their inhabitants as well off as most English cottagers. They are built of mud walls eighteen inches or two feet thick, and well thatched, which are far warmer than the thin clay walls in England. Here are few cottars without a cow, and some of them two. A bellyful invariably of potatoes, and generally turf for fuel from a bog. It is true they have not always chimneys to their cabins, the door serving for that and window too. If their eyes are not affected with the smoke, it may be an advantage in warmth. Every cottage swarms with poultry, and most of them have pigs.

Went in the evening to Lord Mornington's at Dangan, who is making many improvements, which he showed me. His plantations are extensive, and he has formed a large water, having five or six islands much varied, and promontories of high land shoot so far into it as to form almost distant lakes; the effect pleasing. There are above a hundred acres under water, and his lordship has planned a considerable addition to it. Returned to Summerhill.

June 29. Left it, taking the road to Slaine, the country very pleasant all the way; much of it on the banks of the Boyne, variegated with some woods, planted hedgerows, and gentle hills. The cabins continue much the same, the same plenty of poultry, pigs, and cows. The cattle in the road have their fore legs all tied together with straw to keep them from breaking into the fields; even sheep, and pigs, are all in the same bondage.

Lord Conyngham's seat, Slaine Castle, on the Boyne, is one of the most beautiful places I have seen; the grounds are very bold and various, rising round the castle in noble hills or beautiful inequalities of surface, with an outline of flourishing plantations. Under the castle flows the Boyne, in a reach broken by islands, with a very fine shore of rock on one side, and wood on the other. Through the lower plantations are ridings, which look upon several beautiful scenes formed by the river, and take in the distant country, exhibiting the noblest views of waving Cultinald hills, with the castle finely situated in the midst of the planted domain, through which the Boyne winds its beautiful course.

Under Mr. Lambert's house on the same river is a most romantic and beautiful spot; rocks on the side, rising in peculiar forms very boldly; the other steep wood, the river bending short between them like a land-locked basin.

Lord Conyngham's keeping up Slaine Castle, and spending great sums, though he rarely resides there, is an instance of magnificence not often met with; while it is so common for absentees to drain the kingdom of every shilling they can, so contrary a conduct ought to be held in the estimation which it justly deserves.

June 30. Rode out to view the country and some improvements in the neighbourhood: the principal of which are those of Lord Chief Baron Foster, which I saw from Glaston hill, in the road from Slaine to Dundalk.

In conversation with Lord Longford I made many inquiries concerning the state of the lower classes, and found that in some respects they were in good circumstances, in others indifferent; they have, generally speaking, such plenty of potatoes as always to command a bellyful; they have flax enough for all their linen, most of them have a cow, and some two, and spin wool enough for their clothes; all a pig, and numbers of poultry, and in general the complete family of cows, calves, hogs, poultry, and children pig together in the cabin; fuel they have in the utmost plenty. Great numbers of families are also supported by the neighbouring lakes, which abound prodigiously with fish. A child with a packthread and a crooked pin will catch perch enough in an hour for the family to live on the whole day, and his lordship has seen five hundred children fishing at the same time, there being no tenaciousness in the proprietors of the lands about a right to the fish. Besides perch, there is pike upwards of five feet long, bream, tench, trout of ten pounds, and as red as salmon, and fine eels. All these are favourable circumstances, and are very conspicuous in the numerous and healthy families among them.

Reverse the medal: they are ill clothed, and make a wretched appearance, and what is worse,

lower classes

Fed but not clothed.

are much oppressed by many who make them pay too dear for keeping a cow, horse, etc. They have a practice also of keeping accounts with the labourers, contriving by that means to let the poor wretches have very little cash for their year's work. This is a great oppression, farmers and gentlemen keeping accounts with the poor is a cruel abuse: so many days' work for a cabin; so many for a potato garden; so many for keeping a horse, and so many for a cow, are clear accounts which a poor man can understand well, but farther it ought never to go; and when he has worked out what he has of this sort, the rest of his work ought punctually to be paid him every Saturday night. Another circumstance mentioned was the excessive practice they have in general of pilfering. They steal everything they can lay their hands on, and I should remark, that this is an account which has been very generally given me: all sorts of iron hinges, chains, locks, keys, etc.; gates will be cut in pieces, and conveyed away in many places as fast as built; trees as big as a man's body, and that would require ten men to move, gone in a night. Lord Longford has had the new wheels of a car stolen as soon as made. Good stones out of a wall will be taken for a fire-hearth, etc., though a breach is made to get at them. In short, everything, and even such as are apparently of no use to them; nor is it easy to catch them, for they never carry their stolen goods home, but to some bog-hole. Turnips are stolen by car-loads, and two acres of wheat plucked off in a night. In short, their pilfering and stealing is a perfect nuisance. How far it is owing to the oppression of laws aimed solely at the religion of these people, how far to the conduct of the gentlemen and farmers, and how far to the mischievous disposition of the people themselves, it is impossible for a passing traveller to ascertain. I am apt to believe that a better system of law and management would have good effects. They are much worse treated than the poor in England, are talked to in more opprobrious terms, and otherwise very much oppressed.

Left Packenham Hall.

Two or three miles from Lord Longford's in the way to Mullingar the road leads up a mountain, and commands an exceeding fine view of Lock Derrevaragh, a noble water eight miles long, and from two miles to half a mile over; a vast reach of it, like a magnificent river, opens as you rise the hill. Afterwards I passed under the principal mountain, which rises abruptly from the lake into the boldest outline imaginable. The water there is very beautiful, filling up the steep vale formed by this and the opposite hills.

Reached Mullingar.

It was one of the fair days. I saw many cows and beasts, and more horses, with some wool. The cattle were of the same breed that I had generally seen in coming through the country.

July 5. Left Mullingar, which is a dirty ugly town, and taking the road to Tullamore, stopped at Lord Belvidere's, with which place I was as much struck as with any I had ever seen. The house is perched on the crown of a very beautiful little hill, half surrounded with others, variegated and melting into one another. It is one of the most singular places that is anywhere to be seen, and spreading to the eye a beautiful lawn of undulating ground margined with wood. Single trees are scattered in some places, and clumps in others; the general effect so pleasing, that were there nothing further, the place would be beautiful, but the canvas is admirably filled. Lake Ennel, many miles in length, and two or three broad, flows beneath the windows. It is spotted with islets, a promontory of rock fringed with trees shoots into it, and the whole is bounded by distant hills. Greater and more magnificent scenes are often met with, but nowhere a more beautiful or a more singular one.

From Mullingar to Tullespace I found rents in general at twenty shillings an acre, with much relet at thirty shillings, yet all the crops except bere were very bad, and full of weeds. About the latter-named place the farms are generally from one hundred to three hundred acres; and their course: 1. fallow; 2. bere; 3. oats; 4. oats; 5. oats. Great quantities of potatoes all the way, crops from forty to eighty barrels.

The road before it comes to Tullamore leads through a part of the bog of Allen, which seems here extensive, and would make a noble tract of meadow. The way the road was made over it was simply to cut a drain on each side, and then lay on the gravel, which, as fast as it was laid and spread, bore the ears. Along the edges is fine white clover.

In conversation upon the subject of a union with Great Britain, I was informed that nothing was so unpopular in Ireland as such an idea; and that the great objection to it was increasing the number of absentees. When it was in agitation, twenty peers and sixty commoners were talked of to sit in the British Parliament, which would be the resident of eighty of the best estates in Ireland. Going every year to England would, by degrees, make them residents; they would educate their children there, and in time become mere absentees: becoming so they would be unpopular, others would be elected, who, treading in the same steps, would yield the place still to others; and thus by degrees, a vast portion of the kingdom now resident would be made absentees, which would, they think, be so great a drain to Ireland, that a free trade would not repay it.

I think the idea is erroneous, were it only for one circumstance, the kingdom would lose, according to this reasoning, an idle race of country gentlemen, and in exchange their ports would fill with ships and commerce, and all the consequences of commerce, an exchange that never yet proved disadvantageous to any country.

Viewed Mount Juliet, Lord Carrick's seat, which is beautifully situated on a fine declivity on the banks of the Nore, commanding some extensive plantations that spread over the hills, which rise in a various manner on the other side of the river. A knoll of lawn rises among them with artificial ruins upon it, but the situation is not in unison with the idea of a ruin, very rarely placed to effect, unless in retired and melancholy spots.

The river is a very fine one, and has a good accompaniment of well grown wood. From the cottage a more varied scene is viewed, cheering and pleasing; and from the tent in the farther plantation a yet gayer one, which looks down on several bends of the river.

July 11. Left Kilsaine. Mr. Bushe accompanied me to Woodstock, the seat of Sir W. Fownes. From Thomastown hither is the finest ride I have yet had in Ireland. The road leaving Thomastown leads on the east side of the river, through some beautiful copse woods, which before they were cut must have had a most noble effect, with the river Nore winding at the bottom. The country then opens somewhat, and you pass most of the way for six or seven miles to Innisteague, on a declivity shelving down to the river, which takes a varied winding course, sometimes lively, breaking over a rocky bottom, at others still and deep under the gloom of some fine woods, which hang down the sides of steep hills. Narrow slips of meadow of a beautiful verdure in some places form the shore, and unite with cultivated fields that spread over the adjoining hills, reaching almost the mountain tops. These are large and bold, and give in general to the scenes features of great magnificence. Passed Sir John Hasler's on the opposite side of the river, finely situated, and Mr. Nicholson's farm on this side, who has very extensive copses which line the river. Coming in sight of Sir W. Fownes's, the scenery is striking; the road mounts the side of the hill, and commands the river at the bottom of the declivity, with groups of trees prettily scattered about, and the little borough of Innisteague in a most picturesque situation, the whole bounded by mountains. Cross the bridge, and going through the town, take a path that leads to a small building in the woods, called Mount Sandford. It is at the top of a rocky declivity almost perpendicular, but with brush wood growing from the rocks. At the bottom is the river, which comes from the right from behind a very bold hanging wood, that seems to unite with the hill on the opposite shore. At this pass the river fills the vale, but it widens by degrees, and presents various reaches, intermixed with little tufts of trees. The bridge we passed over is half hid. Innisteague is mixed with them, and its buildings backed by a larger wood, give variety to the scene. Opposite to the point of view there are some pretty enclosures, fringed with wood, and a line of cultivated mountain sides, with their bare tops limit the whole.

Taking my leave of Mr. Bushe, I followed the road to Ross. Passed Woodstock, of which there is a very fine view from the top of one of the hills, the house in the centre of a sloping wood of five hundred English acres, and hanging in one noble shade to the river, which flows at the bottom of a winding glen. From the same hill in front it is seen in a winding course for many miles through a great extent of enclosures, bounded by mountains. As I advanced the views of the river Nore were very fine, till I came to Ross, where from the hill before you go down to the ferry is a noble scene of the Barrow, a vast river flowing through bold shores. In some places trees on the bank half obscure it, in others it opens in large reaches, the effect equally grand and beautiful. Ships sailing up to the town, which is built on the side of a hill to the water's edge, enliven the scene not a little. The water is very deep and the navigation secure, so that ships of seven hundred tons may come up to the town; but these noble harbours on the coast of Ireland are only melancholy capabilities of commerce: it is languid and trifling. There are only four or five brigs and sloops that belong to the place.

Having now passed through a considerable extent of country, in which the Whiteboys were common, and committed many outrages, I shall here review the intelligence I received concerning them throughout the county of Kilkenny. I made many inquiries into the origin of those disturbances, and found that no such thing as a leveller or Whiteboy was heard of till 1760, which was long after the landing of Thurot, or the intending expedition of M. Conflans. That no foreign coin was ever seen among them, though reports to the contrary were circulated; and in all the evidence that was taken during ten or twelve years, in which time there appeared a variety of informers, none was ever taken, whose testimony could be relied on, that ever proved any foreign interposition. Those very few who attempted to favour it, were of the most infamous and

Whiteboys

perjured characters. All the rest, whose interest it was to make the discovery, if they had known it, and who concealed nothing else, pretended to no such knowledge. No foreign money appeared, no arms of foreign construction, no presumptive proof whatever of such a connection. They began in Tipperary, and were owing to some inclosures of commons, which they threw down, levelling the ditches, and were first known by the name of Levellers. After that, they began with the tithe-proctors (who are men that hire tithes of the rectors), and these proctors either screwed the cottars up to the utmost shilling, or relet the tithes to such as did it. It was a common practice with them to go in parties about the country, swearing many to be true to them, and forcing them to join by menaces, which they very often carried into execution. At last they set up to be general redressers of grievances, punished all obnoxious persons who advanced the value of lands, or hired farms over their heads; and, having taken the administration of justice into their hands, were not very exact in the distribution of it. Forced masters to release their apprentices, carried off the daughters of rich farmers, and ravished them into marriages, of which four instances happened in a fortnight. They levied sums of money on the middling and lower farmers in order to support their cause, by paying attorneys, etc., in defending prosecutions against them; and many of them subsisted for some years without work, supported by these contributions. Sometimes they committed several considerable robberies, breaking into houses, and taking the money, under pretence of redressing grievances. In the course of these outrages they burnt several houses, and destroyed the whole substance of men obnoxious to them. The barbarities they committed were shocking. One of their usual punishments (and by no means the most severe) was taking people out of their beds, carrying them naked in winter on horseback for some distance, and burying them up to their chin in a hole filled with briars, not forgetting to cut off their ears. In this manner the evil existed for eight or ten years, during which time the gentlemen of the country took some measures to quell them. Many of the magistrates were active in apprehending them; but the want of evidence prevented punishments, for many of those who even suffered by them had no spirit to prosecute. The gentlemen of the country had frequent expeditions to discover them in arms; but their intelligence was so uncommonly good by their influence over the common people, that not one party that ever went out in quest of them was successful. Government offered large rewards for informations, which brought a few every year to the gallows, without any radical cure for the evil. The reason why it was not more effective was the necessity of any person that gave evidence against them quitting their houses and country, or remaining exposed to their resentment. At last their violence arose to a height which brought on their suppression. The popish inhabitants of Ballyragget, six miles from Kilkenny, were the first of the lower people who dared openly to associate against them; they threatened destruction to the town, gave notice that they would attack it, were as good as their word, came two hundred strong, drew up before a house in which were fifteen armed men, and fired in at the windows; the fifteen men handled their arms so well, that in a few rounds they killed forty or fifty. They fled immediately, and ever after left Ballyragget in peace: indeed, they have never been resisted at all without showing a great want of both spirit and discipline. It should, however, be observed, that they had but very few arms, those in bad order, and no cartridges. Soon after this they attacked the house of Mr. Power in Tipperary, the history of which is well known. His murder spirited up the gentlemen to exert themselves in suppressing the evil, especially in raising subscriptions to give private rewards to whoever would give evidence or information concerning them. The private distribution had much more effect than larger sums which required a public declaration; and Government giving rewards to those who resisted them, without having previously promised it, had likewise some effect. Laws were passed for punishing all who assembled, and (what may have a great effect) for recompensing, at the expense of the county or barony, all persons who suffered by their outrages. In consequence of this general exertion, above twenty were capitally convicted, and most of them executed; and the gaols of this and the three neighbouring counties, Carlow, Tipperary, and Queen's County, have many in them whose trials are put off till next assizes, and against whom sufficient evidence for conviction, it is supposed, will appear. Since this all has been quiet, and no outrages have been committed: but before I quit the subject, it is proper to remark that what coincided very much to abate the evil was the fall in the price of lands which has taken place lately. This is considerable, and has much lessened the evil of hiring farms over the heads of one another; perhaps, also, the tithe-proctors have not been quite so severe in their extortions: but this observation is by no means general; for in many places tithes yet continue to be levied with all those circumstances which originally raised the evil.

July 15. Leaving Courtown, took the Arklow road; passed a finely wooded park of Mr. Ram's, and a various country with some good corn in it. Flat lands by the coast let very high, and mountain at six or seven shillings an acre, and some at eight shillings or ten shillings. Passed to Wicklow, prettily situated on the sea, and from Newrybridge walked to see Mr. Tye's, which is a neat farm, well wooded, with a river running through the fields.

Reached in the evening Mount Kennedy, the seat of General Cunninghame, who fortunately proved to me an instructor as assiduous as he is able. He is in the midst of a country almost his own, for he has 10,000 Irish acres here. His domain, and the grounds about it, are very beautiful; not a level can be seen; every spot is tossed about in a variety of hill and dale. In the middle of the lawn is one of the greatest natural curiosities in the kingdom: an immense arbutus tree, unfortunately blown down, but yet vegetating. One branch, which parts from the body near the ground, and afterwards into many large branches, is six feet two inches in circumference. The General buried part of the stem as it laid, and it is from several branches throwing out fine young shoots: it is a most venerable remnant. Killarney, the region of the arbutus, boasts of no such tree as this.

July 16. Rode in the morning to Drum; a large extent of mountains and wood on the General's estate. It is a very noble scenery; a vast rocky glen; one side bare rocks to an immense height, hanging in a thousand whimsical yet frightful forms, with vast fragments tumbled from them, and lying in romantic confusion; the other a fine mountain side covered with shrubby wood. This wild pass leads to the bottom of an amphitheatre of mountain, which exhibits a very noble scenery. To the right is an immense sweep of mountain completely wooded; taken as a single object it is a most magnificent one, but its forms are picturesque in the highest degree; great projections of hill, with glens behind all wooded, have a noble effect. Every feature of the whole view is great, and unites to form a scene of natural magnificence. From hence a riding is cut through the hanging wood, which rises to a central spot, where the General has cleared away the rubbish from under the wood, and made a beautiful waving lawn with many oaks and hollies scattered about it: here he has built a cottage, a pretty, whimsical oval room, from the windows of which are three views, one of distant rich lands opening to the sea, one upon a great mountain, and a third upon a part of the lawn. It is well placed, and forms upon the whole a most agreeable retreat.

July 17. Took my leave of General Cunninghame, and went through the glen of the downs in my way to Powerscourt. The glen is a pass between two vast ridges of mountains covered with wood, which have a very noble effect. The vale is no wider than to admit the road, a small gurgling river almost by its side, and narrow slips of rocky and shrubby ground which part them. In the front all escape seems denied by an immense conical mountain, which rises out of the glen and seems to fill it up. The scenery is of a most magnificent character. On the top of the ridge to the right Mr. La Touche has a banqueting-room. Passing from this sublime scene, the road leads through cheerful grounds all under corn, rising and falling to the eye, and then to a vale of charming verdure broken into inclosures, and bounded by two rocky mountains, distant darker mountains filling up the scene in front. This whole ride is interesting, for within a mile and a half of "Tinnyhinch" (the inn to which I was directed), you come to a delicious view on the right: a small vale opening to the sea, bounded by mountains, whose dark shade forms a perfect contrast to the extreme beauty and lively verdure of the lower scene, consisting of gently swelling lawns rising from each other, with groups of trees between, and the whole so prettily scattered with white farms, as to add every idea of cheerfulness. Kept on towards Powerscourt, which presently came in view from the edge of a declivity. You look full upon the house, which appears to be in the most beautiful situation in the world, on the side of a mountain, half-way between its bare top and an irriguous vale at its foot. In front, and spreading among woods on either side, is a lawn whose surface is beautifully varied in gentle declivities, hanging to a winding river.

Lowering the hill the scenery is yet more agreeable. The near inclosures are margined with trees, through whose open branches are seen whole fields of the most lively verdure. The trees gather into groups, and the lawn swells into gentle inequalities, while the river winding beneath renders the whole truly pleasing.

Breakfasted at the inn at Tinnyhinch, and then drove to the park to see the waterfall. The park itself is fine; you enter it between two vast masses of mountain, covered with wood, forming a vale scattered with trees, through which flows a river on a broken rocky channel. You follow this vale till it is lost in a most uncommon manner; the ridges of mountain, closing, form one great amphitheatre of wood, from the top of which, at the height of many hundred feet, bursts the water from a rock, and tumbling down the side of a very large one, forms a scene singularly beautiful. At the bottom is a spot of velvet turf, from which rises a clump of oaks, and through their stems, branches and leaves, the falling water is seen as a background, with an effect more picturesque than can be well imagined. These few trees, and this little lawn, give the finishing to the scene. The water falls behind some large fragments of rock, and turns to the left, down a stony channel, under the shade of a wood.

Returning to Tinnyhinch, I went to Inniskerry, and gained by this detour in my return to go to the Dargle, a beautiful view which I should otherwise have lost. The road runs on the edge of a declivity, from whence there is a most pleasing prospect of the river's course through the vale and the wood of Powerscourt, which here appear in large masses of dark shade, the whole bounded by mountains. Turn to the left into the private road that leads to the Dargle, and presently it gives a specimen of what is to be expected by a romantic glen of wood, where the high lands almost lock into each other, and leave scarce a passage for the river at bottom, which rages as if with difficulty forcing its way. It is topped by a high mountain, and in front you catch a beautiful plat of inclosures bounded by the sea. Enter the Dargle, which is the name of a glen near a mile long, come presently to one of the finest ranges of wood I have anywhere seen. It is a narrow glen or vale formed by the sides of two opposite mountains; the whole thickly spread with oak wood. At the bottom (and the depth is immense), it is narrowed to the mere channel of the river, which rather tumbles from rock to rock than runs. The extent of wood that hangs to the eye in every direction is great, the depth of the precipice on which you stand immense, which with the roar of the water at bottom forms a scene truly interesting. In less than a quarter of a mile, the road passing through the wood leads to another point of view to the right. It is the crown of a vast projecting rock, from which you look down a precipice absolutely perpendicular, and many hundred feet deep, upon the torrent at the bottom, which finds its noisy way over large fragments of rock. The point of view is a great projection of the mountain on this side, answered by a concave of the opposite, so that you command the glen both to the right and left. It exhibits on both immense sheets of forest, which have a most magnificent appearance. Beyond the wood to the right, are some inclosures hanging on the side of a hill, crowned by a mountain. I knew not how to leave so interesting a spot; the impressions raised by it are strong. The solemnity of such an extent of wood unbroken by any intervening objects, and the whole hanging over declivities, is alone great; but to this the addition of a constant roar of falling water, either quite hid, or so far below as to be seen but obscurely, united to make those impressions stronger. No contradictory emotions are raised; no ill-judged temples appear to enliven a scene that is gloomy rather than gay. Falling or moving water is a lively object; but this being obscure the noise operates differently. Following the road a little further, there is another bold rocky projection from which also there is a double view to the right and left. In front so immense a sweep of hanging wood, that a nobler scene can hardly be imagined; the river as before, at the bottom of the precipice, which is so steep and the depth so great as to be quite fearful to look down. This horrid precipice, the pointed bleak mountains in view, with the roar of the water, all conspire to raise one great emotion of the sublime. You advance scarcely twenty yards before a pretty scene opens to the left—a distant landscape of inclosures, with a river winding between the hills to the sea. Passing to the right, fresh scenes of wood appear; half-way to the bottom, one different from the preceding is seen; you are almost inclosed in wood, and look to the right through some low oaks on the opposite bank of wood, with an edging of trees through which the sky is seen, which, added to an uncommon elegance in the outline of the hill, has a most pleasing effect. Winding down to a thatched bench on a rocky point, you look upon an uncommon scene. Immediately beneath is a vast chasm in the rock, which seems torn asunder to let the torrent through that comes tumbling over a rocky bed far sunk into a channel embosomed in wood. Above is a range of gloomy obscure woods, which half overshadow it, and rising to a vast height, exclude every object. To the left the water rolls away over broken rocks—a scene duly romantic. Followed the path: it led me to the water's edge, at the bottom of the glen, where is a new scene, in which not a single circumstance hurts the principal character. In a hollow formed of rock and wood (every object excluded but those and water) the torrent breaks forth from fragments of rock, and tumbles through the chasm, rocks bulging over it as if ready to fall into the channel and stop the impetuous water. The shade is so thick as to exclude the heavens; all is retired and gloomy, a brown horror breathing over the whole. It is a spot for melancholy to muse in.

Return to the carriage, and quit the Dargle, which upon the whole is a very singular place, different from all I have seen in England, and I think preferable to most. Cross a murmuring stream, clear as crystal, and, rising a hill, look back on a pleasing landscape of inclosures, which, waving over hills, end in mountains of a very noble character. Reach Dublin.

July 20. To Drogheda, a well-built town, active in trade, the Boyne bringing ships to it. It was market-day, and I found the quantity of corn, etc., and the number of people assembled, very great; few country markets in England more thronged. The Rev. Mr. Nesbit, to whom recommended, absent, which was a great loss to me, as I had several inquiries which remained unsatisfied.

To the field of battle on the Boyne. The view of the scene from a rising ground which looks down upon it is exceedingly beautiful, being one of the completest landscapes I have seen. It is a vale, losing itself in front between bold declivities, above which are some thick woods and distant country. Through the vale the river winds and forms an island, the point of which is tufted with trees in the prettiest manner imaginable; on the other side a rich scenery of wood, among which is Dr. Norris's house. To the right, on a rising ground on the banks of the river, is the obelisk, backed by a very bold declivity. Pursued the road till near it, quitted my chaise, and walked to the foot of it. It is founded on a rock which rises boldly from the river. It is a noble pillar, and admirably placed. I seated myself on the opposite rock, and indulged the emotions which, with a melancholy not unpleasing, filled my bosom, while I reflected on the consequences that had sprung from the victory here obtained. Liberty was then triumphant. May the virtues of our posterity secure that prize which the bravery of their ancestors won! Peace to the memory of the Prince to whom, whatever might be his failings, we owed that day memorable in the annals of Europe!

Returned part of the way, and took the road to Cullen, where the Lord Chief Baron Forster received me in the most obliging manner, and gave me a variety of information uncommonly valuable. He has made the greatest improvements I have anywhere met with. The whole

Boyne.

country twenty-two years ago was a waste sheep-walk, covered chiefly with heath, with some dwarf furze and fern. The cabins and people as miserable as can be conceived; not a Protestant in the country, nor a road passable for a carriage. In a word, perfectly resembling other mountainous tracts, and the whole yielding a rent of not more than from three shillings to four shillings an acre. Mr. Forster could not bear so barren a property, and determined to attempt the improvement of an estate of five thousand acres till then deemed irreclaimable. He encouraged the tenants by every species of persuasion and expense, but they had so ill an opinion of the land that he was forced to begin with two or three thousand acres in his own hands; he did not, however, turn out the people, but kept them in to see the effects of his operations.

To Dundalk. The view down on this town also very beautiful: swelling hills of a fine verdure, with many rich inclosures backed by a bold outline of mountain that is remarkable. Laid at the Clanbrassil Arms, and found it a very good inn. The place, like most of the Irish towns I have been in, full of new buildings, with every mark of increasing wealth and prosperity. A cambric manufacture was established here by Parliament, but failed; it was, however, the origin of that more to the north.

July 22. Left Dundalk, took the road through Ravensdale to Mr. Fortescue, to whom I had a letter, but unfortunately he was in the South of Ireland. Here I saw many good stone and slate houses, and some bleach greens; and I was much pleased to see the inclosures creeping high up the sides of the mountains, stony as they are. Mr. Fortescue's situation is very romantic—on the side of a mountain, with fine wood hanging on every side, with the lawn beautifully scattered with trees spreading into them, and a pretty river winding through the vale, beautiful in itself, but trebly so on information that before he fixed there it was all a wild waste. Rents in Ravensdale ten shillings; mountain land two shillings and sixpence to five shillings. Also large tracts rented by villages, the cottars dividing it among themselves, and making the mountain common for their cattle.

Breakfasted at Newry—the Globe, another good inn. This town appears exceedingly flourishing, and is very well built; yet forty years ago, I was told, there were nothing but mud cabins in it. This great rise has been much owing to the canal to Loch Neagh. I crossed it twice; it is indeed a noble work. I was amazed to see ships of one hundred and fifty tons and more lying in it, like barges in an English canal. Here is a considerable trade.

Reached Armagh in the evening, and waited on the Primate.

July 23. His Grace rode out with me to Armagh, and showed me some of the noble and spirited works by which he has perfectly changed the face of the neighbourhood. The buildings he has erected in seven years, one would suppose, without previous information, to be the work of an active life. A list of them will justify this observation.

He has erected a very elegant palace, ninety feet by sixty, and forty high, in which an unadorned simplicity reigns. It is light and pleasing, without the addition of wings or lesser parts, which too frequently wanting a sufficient uniformity with the body of the edifice, are unconnected with it in effect, and divide the attention. Large and ample offices are conveniently placed behind a plantation at a small distance. Around the palace is a large lawn, which spreads on every side over the hills, and is skirted by young plantations, in one of which is a terrace, which commands a most beautiful view of cultivated hill and dale. The view from the palace is much improved by the barracks, the school, and a new church at a distance, all which are so placed as to be exceedingly ornamental to the whole country.

The barracks were erected under his Grace's directions, and form a large and handsome edifice. The school is a building of considerable extent, and admirably adapted for the purpose: a more convenient or a better contrived one is nowhere to be seen. There are apartments for a master, a school-room fifty-six feet by twenty-eight, a large dining-room, and spacious, airy dormitories, with every other necessary, and a spacious playground walled in; the whole forming a handsome front: and attention being paid to the residence of the master (the salary is four hundred pounds a year), the school flourishes, and must prove one of the greatest advantages to the country of anything that could have been established. This edifice entirely at the Primate's expense. The church is erected of white stone, and having a tall spire makes a very agreeable object in a country where churches and spires do not abound—at least, such as are worth looking at. Three other churches the Primate has also built, and done considerable reparations to the cathedral.

He has been the means also of erecting a public infirmary, which was built by subscription, contributing amply to it himself.

A public library he has erected at his own expense, given a large collection of books, and endowed it. The room is excellently adapted, forty-five feet by twenty-five, and twenty high, with a gallery, and apartments for a librarian.

He has further ornamented the city with a market-house and shambles, and been the direct means, by giving leases upon that condition, of almost new-building the whole place. He found it a nest of mud cabins, and he will leave it a well-built city of stone and slate. I heard it asserted in common conversation that his Grace, in these noble undertakings, had not expended less than thirty thousand pounds, besides what he had been the means of doing, though not directly at his own expense.

In the evening reached Mr. Brownlow's at Lurgan, to whom I am indebted for some valuable information. This gentleman has made very great improvements in his domain. He has a lake at the bottom of a slight vale, and around are three walks, at a distance from each other; the centre one is the principal, and extends two miles. It is well conducted for leading to the most agreeable parts of the grounds, and for commanding views of Loch Neagh, and the distant country. There are several buildings, a temple, green-house, etc. The most beautiful scene is from a bench on a gently swelling hill, which rises almost on every side from the water. The wood, the water, and the green slopes, here unite to form a very pleasing landscape. Let me observe one thing much to his honour; he advances his tenants money for all the lime they choose, and takes payment in eight years with rent.

Upon inquiring concerning the emigrations, I found that in 1772 and 1773 they were at the height; that some went from this neighbourhood with property, but not many. They were in general poor and unemployed. They find here that when provisions are very cheap, the poor spend much of their time in whisky-houses. All the drapers wish that oatmeal was never under one penny a pound. Though farms are exceedingly divided, yet few of the people raise oatmeal enough to feed themselves; all go to market for some. The weavers earn by coarse linens one shilling a day, by fine one shilling and fourpence, and it is the same with the spinners—the finer the yarn, the more they earn; but in common a woman earns about threepence. For coarse linens they do not reckon the flax hurt by standing for seed. Their own flax is much better than the imported.

This country is in general beautiful, but particularly so about the straits that lead into Strangford Loch. From Mr. Savage's door the view has great variety. To the left are tracts of hilly grounds, between which the sea appears, and the vast chain of mountains in the Isle of Man distinctly seen. In front the hills rise in a beautiful outline, and a round hill projects like a promontory into the strait, and under it the town amidst groups of trees; the scene is cheerful of itself, but rendered doubly so by the ships and herring-boats sailing in and out. To the right the view is crowned by the mountains of Mourne, which, wherever seen, are of a character peculiarly bold, and even terrific. The shores of the loch behind Mr. Savage's are bold ground, abounding with numerous pleasing landscapes; the opposite coast, consisting of the woods and improvements of Castle Ward, is a fine scenery.

Called at Lord Bangor's, at Castle Ward, to deliver a letter of recommendations but unfortunately he was on a sailing party to England; walked through the woods, etc. The house was built by the present lord. It is a very handsome edifice, with two principal fronts, but not of the same architecture, for the one is Gothic and the other Grecian. From the temple is a fine wooded scene: you look down on a glen of wood, with a winding hill quite covered with it, and which breaks the view of a large bay. Over it appears the peninsula of Strangford, which consists of enclosures and wood. To the right the bay is bounded by a fine grove, which projects into it. A ship at anchor added much. The house well situated above several rising woods; the whole scene a fine one. I remarked in Lord Bangor's domains a fine field of turnips, but unhoed. There were some cabbages also.

Belfast is a very well built town of brick, they having no stone quarry in the neighbourhood. The streets are broad and straight, and the inhabitants, amounting to about fifteen thousand, make it appear lively and busy. The public buildings are not numerous nor very striking, but over the exchange Lord Donegal is building an assembly room, sixty feet long by thirty broad, and twenty-four high; a very elegant room. A card-room adjoining, thirty by twenty-two, and twenty-two high; a tea-room of the same size. His lordship is also building a new church, which is one of the lightest and most pleasing I have anywhere seen: it is seventy-four by fifty-four, and thirty high to the cornice, the aisles separated by a double row of columns; nothing can be lighter or more pleasing. The town belongs entirely to his lordship. Rent of it £2,000 a year. His estate extends from Drumbridge, near Lisburn, to Larne, twenty miles in a right line, and is ten broad. His royalties are great, containing the whole of Loch Neagh, which is, I suppose, the greatest of any subject in Europe. His eel fishery at Tome, and Port New, on the river Ban, lets for £500 a year; and all the fisheries are his to the leap at Coleraine. The estate is supposed to be £31,000 a year, the greatest at present in Ireland. Inishowen, in Donegal, is his, and is £11,000 of it. In Antrim, Lord Antrim's is the most extensive property, being four baronies, and one hundred and seventy-three thousand acres. The rent £8,000 a year, but re-let for £64,000 a year, by tenants that have perpetuities, perhaps the cruellest instance in the world of carelessness for the interests of posterity. The present lord's father granted those leases.

I was informed that Mr. Isaac, near Belfast, had four acres, Irish measure, of strong clay land not broken up for many years, which being amply manured with lime rubbish and sea shells, and fallowed, was sown with wheat, and yielded £87 9s. at 9s. to 12s. per cwt. Also that Mr. Whitley, of Ballinderry, near Lisburn, a tenant of Lord Hertford's, has rarely any wheat that does not yield him £18 an acre. The tillage of the neighbourhood for ten miles round is doubled in a few years. Shall export one thousand tons of corn this year from Belfast, most of it to the West Indies, particularly oats.

August 1. To Arthur Buntin's, Esq., near Belfast; the soil a stiff clay; lets at old rents 10s., new one 18s., the town parks of that place 30s. to 70s., ten miles round it 10s. to 20s., average 13s. A great deal of flax sown, every countryman having a little, always on potato land, and one ploughing: they usually sow each family a bushel of seed. Those who have no land pay the farmers 20s. rent for the land a bushel of seed sows, and always on potato land. They plant many more potatoes than they eat, to supply the market at Belfast; manure for them with all their dung, and some of them mix dung, earth, and lime, and this is found to do better. There is much alabaster near the town, which is used for stucco plaster; sells from £1 1s. to 25s. a ton.

On my way to Antrim, viewed the bleach green of Mr. Thomas Sinclair; it is the completest I have seen here. I understood that the bleaching season lasted nine months, and that watering on the grass was quite left off. Mr. Sinclair himself was not at home, or I should probably have gained some intelligence that might have been useful.

Crossed the mountains by the new road to Antrim, and found them to the summits to consist of exceeding good loam, and such as would improve into good meadow. It is all thrown to the little adjoining farms, with very little or any rent paid for it. They make no other use of it than turning their cows on. Pity they do not improve; a work more profitable than any they could undertake. All the way to Antrim lands let, at an average, at 8s. The linen manufacture spreads over the whole country, consequently the farms are very small, being nothing but patches for the convenience of weavers.

From Antrim to Shanes Castle the road runs at the end of Loch Neagh, commanding a noble view of it; of such an extent that the eye can see no land over it. It appears like a perfect sea, and the shore is broken sand-banks, which look so much like it, that one can hardly believe the water to be fresh. Upon my arrival at the castle, I was most agreeably saluted with four men hoeing a field of turnips round it, as a preparation for grass. These were the first turnip-hoers I have seen in Ireland, and I was more pleased than if I had seen four emperors.

The castle is beautifully situated on the lake, the windows commanding a very noble view of it; and this has the finer effect, as the woods are considerable, and form a fine accompaniment to this noble inland sea.

Rode from Mr. Lesly's to view the Giant's Causeway. It is certainly a very great curiosity as an object for speculation upon the manner of its formation; whether it owes its origin to fire, and is a species of lava, or to crystallisation, or to whatever cause, is a point that has employed the attention of men much more able to decide upon it than I am; and has been so often treated, that nothing I could say could be new. When two bits of these basalts are rubbed together quick, they emit a considerable scent like burnt leather. The scenery of the Causeway, nor of the adjacent mountains, is very magnificent, though the cliffs are bold; but for a considerable distance there is a strong disposition in the rocks to run into pentagonal cylinders, and even at a bridge by Mr. Lesly's is a rock in which the same disposition is plainly visible. I believe the Causeway would have struck me more if I had not seen the prints of Staffa.

Returned to Lesly Hill, and on August 5th departed for Coleraine. There the Right Hon. Mr. Jackson assisted me with the greatest politeness in procuring the intelligence I wished about the salmon fishery, which is the greatest in the kingdom, and viewed both fisheries, above and below the town, very pleasantly situated on the river Ban. The salmon spawn in all the rivers that run into the Ban about the beginning of August, and as soon as they have done, swim to the sea, where they stay till January, when they begin to return to the fresh water, and continue doing it till August, in which voyage they are taken. The nets are set in the middle of January, but by Act of Parliament no nets nor weirs can be kept down after the 12th of August. All the fisheries on the river Ban let at £6,000 a year. From the sea to the rock above Coleraine, where the weirs are built, belongs to the London companies; the greatest part of the rest to Lord Donegal. The eel fisheries let at £1,000 a year, and the salmon fisheries at Coleraine at £1,000. The eels make periodical voyages, as the salmon, but instead of spawning in the fresh water, they go to the sea to spawn, and the young fry return against the stream; to enable them to do which with greater ease at the leap straw ropes are hung in the water for them. When they return to sea they are taken. Many of them weigh nine or ten pounds. The young salmon are called grawls, and grow at a rate which I should suppose scarce any fish commonly known equals; for within the year some of them will come to sixteen and eighteen pounds, but in general ten or twelve pounds. Such as escape the first year's fishery are salmon; and at two years old will generally weigh twenty to twenty-five pounds. This year's fishery has proved the greatest that ever was known, and they had the largest haul, taking 1,452 salmon at one drag of one net. In the year 1758 they had 882, which was the next greatest haul. I had the pleasure of seeing 370 drawn in at once. They have this year taken 400 tons of fish; 200 sold fresh at a penny and three-halfpence a pound, and two hundred salted, at £18 and £20 per ton, which are sent to London, Spain, and Italy. The fishery employs eighty men, and the expenses in general are calculated to equal the rent.

The linen manufacture is very general about Coleraine, coarse ten-hundred linen. It is carried to Dublin in cars, one hundred and ten miles, at 5s. per cwt. in summer, and 7s. 6d. in winter.

From Limavady to Derry there is very little uncultivated land. Within four miles of the latter, rents are from 12s. to 20s.; mountains paid for but in the gross. Reached Derry at night, and waited two hours in the dark before the ferry-boat came over for me.

August 7. In the morning went to the bishop's palace to leave my letters of recommendation; for I was informed of my misfortune in his being out of the kingdom. He was upon a voyage to Staffa, and had sent home some of the stones of which it consists. They appeared perfectly to resemble in shape, colour, and smell, those of the Giant's Causeway.

August 8. Left Derry, and took the road by Raphoe to the Rev. Mr. Golding's at Clonleigh, who favoured me with much valuable information. The view of Derry at the distance of a mile or two is the most picturesque of any place I have seen. It seems to be built on an island of bold land rising from the river, which spreads into a fine basin at the foot of the town; the adjacent country hilly. The scene wants nothing but wood to make it a perfect landscape.

August 11. Left Mount Charles, and passing through Donegal took the road to Ballyshannon; came presently to several beautiful landscapes, swelling hills cultivated, with the bay flowing up among them. They want nothing but more wood, and are beautiful without it. Afterwards likewise to the left they rise in various outlines, and die away insensibly into one another. When the road leads to a full view of the bay of Donegal, these smiling spots, above which the proud mountains rear their heads, are numerous, the hillocks of almost regular circular forms. They are very pleasing from form, verdure, and the water breaking in their vales.

Before I got to Ballyshannon, remarked a bleach green, which indicates weaving in the neighbourhood. Viewed the salmon-leap at Ballyshannon, which is let for £400 a year. The scenery of it is very beautiful. It is a fine fall, and the coast of the river very bold, consisting of perpendicular rocks with grass of a beautiful verdure to the very edge. It projects in little promontories, which grew longer as they approach the sea, and open to give a fine view of the ocean. Before the fall in the middle of the river, is a rocky island on which is a curing house, instead of the turret of a ruined castle for which it seems formed. The town prettily situated on the rising ground on each side of the river. To Sir James Caldwell's. Crossing the bridge, stopped for a view of the river, which is a very fine one, and was delighted to see the salmon jump, to me an unusual sight; the water was perfectly alive with them. Rising the hill, look back on the town; the situation beautiful, the river presents a noble view. Come to Belleek, a little village with one of the finest water-falls I remember anywhere to have seen; viewed it from the bridge. The river in a very broad sheet comes from behind some wood, and breaks over a bed of rocks, not perpendicular, but shelving in various directions, and foams away under the arches, after which it grows more silent and gives a beautiful bend under a rock crowned by a fine bank of wood. Reached Castle Caldwell at night, where Sir James Caldwell received me with a politeness and cordiality that will make me long remember it with pleasure.

August 15. To Belleisle, the charming seat of the Earl of Ross. It is an island in Loch Earne, of two hundred Irish acres, every part of it hill, dale, and gentle declivities; it has a great deal of wood, much of which is old, and forms both deep shades and open, cheerful groves. The trees hang on the slopes, and consequently show themselves to the best advantage. All this is exceedingly pretty, but it is rendered trebly so by the situation. A reach of the lake passes before the house, which is situated near the banks among some fine woods, which give both beauty and shelter. This sheet of water, which is three miles over, is bounded in front by an island of thick wood, and by a bold circular hill which is his lordship's deer park; this hill is backed by a considerable mountain. To the right are four or five fine clumps of dark wood—so many islands which rise boldly from the lake; the water breaks in straits between them, and forms a scene extremely picturesque. On the other side the lake stretches behind wood in a strait which forms Belleisle. Lord Ross has made walks round the island, from which there is a considerable variety of prospect. A temple is built on a gentle hill, commanding the view of the wooded islands above-mentioned, but the most pleasing prospect of them is coming out from the grotto. They appear in an uncommon beauty; two seem to join, and the water which flows between takes the appearance of a fine bay, projecting deep into a dark wood: nothing can be more beautiful. The park hill rises above them, and the whole is backed with mountains. The home scene at your feet also is pretty; a lawn scattered with trees that forms the margin of the lake, closing gradually in a thick wood of tall trees, above the tops of which is a distant view of Cultiegh mountain, which is there seen in its proudest solemnity.

They plough all with horses three or four in a plough, and all abreast. Here let it be remarked that they very commonly plough and harrow with their horses drawing by the tail: it is done every season. Nothing can put them beside this, and they insist that, take a horse tired in traces and put him to work by the tail, he will draw better: quite fresh again. Indignant reader, this is no jest of mine, but cruel, stubborn, barbarous truth. It is so all over Cavan.

At Clonells, near Castlerea, lives O'Connor, the direct descendant of Roderick O'Connor, who was king of Connaught six or seven hundred years ago; there is a monument of him in Roscommon Church, with his sceptre, etc. I was told as a certainty that this family were here long before the coming of the Milesians. Their possessions, formerly so great, are reduced to three or four hundred pounds a year, the family having fared in the revolutions of so many ages much worse than the O'Niels and O'Briens. The common people pay him the greatest respect, and send him presents of cattle, etc., upon various occasions. They consider him as the prince of a people involved in one common ruin.

Another great family in Connaught is Macdermot, who calls himself Prince of Coolavin. He lives at Coolavin, in Sligo, and though he has not above one hundred pounds a year, will not admit his children to sit down in his presence. This was certainly the case with his father, and some assured me even with the present chief. Lord Kingsborough, Mr. Ponsonby, Mr. O'Hara, Mr. Sandford, etc., came to see him, and his address was curious: "O'Hara, you are welcome! Sandford, I am glad to see your mother's son" (his mother was an O'Brien): "as to the rest of ye, come in as ye can." Mr. O'Hara, of Nymphsfield, is in possession of a considerable estate in Sligo, which is the remains of great possessions they had in that country. He is one of the few descendants of the Milesian race.

To Lord Kingston's, to whom I had a letter, but unfortunately for me he was at Spa. Walked down to Longford Hill to view the lake. It is one of the most delicious scenes I ever beheld; a lake of five miles by four, which fills the bottom of a gentle valley almost of a circular form, bounded very boldly by the mountains. Those to the left rise in a noble slope; they lower rather in front, and let in a view of Strand mountain, near Sligo, above twenty miles off. To the right you look over a small part of a bog to a large extent of cultivated hill, with the blue mountains beyond. Were this little piece of bog planted, the view would be more complete; the hill on which you stand has a foliage of well-grown trees, which form the southern shore. You look down on six islands, all wooded, and on a fine promontory to the left, which shoots far into the lake. Nothing can be more pleasing than their uncommon variety. The first is small (Rock Island), tufted with trees, under the shade of which is an ancient building, once the residence of Macdermot. The next a mixture of lawn and wood. The third, which appears to join this, is of a darker shade, yet not so thick but you can see the bright lawn under the trees. House Island is one fine, thick wood, which admits not a gleam of light, a contrast to the silver bosom of the lake. Church Island is at a greater distance; this is also a clump, and rises boldly. Rock Island is of wood; it opens in the centre and shows a lawn with a building on it. It is impossible to imagine a more pleasing and cheerful scene. Passed the chapel to Smithfield Hill, which is a fine rising ground, quite surrounded with plantations. From hence the view is changed; here the promontory appears very bold, and over its neck you see another wooded island in a most picturesque situation. Nothing can be more picturesque than Rock Island, its ruin overhung with ivy. The other islands assume fresh and varied outlines, and form upon the whole one of the most luxuriant scenes I have met with.

The views of the lake and environs are very fine as you go to Boyle; the woods unite into a large mass, and contrast the bright sheet of water with their dark shades.

The lands about Kingston are very fine, a rich, dry, yellow, sandy loam, the finest soil that I have seen in Ireland; all grass, and covered with very fine bullocks, cows, and sheep. The farms rise to five hundred acres, and are generally in divisions, parted by stone walls, for oxen, cows, young cattle, and sheep separate. Some of the lands will carry an ox and a wether per acre; rents, 15s. to 20s.

Dined at Boyle, and took the road to Ballymoat. Crossed an immense mountainy bog, where I stopped and made inquiries; found that it was ten miles long, and three and a half over, containing thirty-five square miles; that limestone quarries were around and in it, and limestone gravel in many places to be found, and used in the lands that join it. In addition to this I may add that there is a great road crossing it. Thirty-five miles are twenty-two thousand four hundred acres. What an immense field of improvement! Nothing would be easier than to drain it (vast tracts of land have such a fall), that not a drop of water could remain. These hilly bogs are extremely different from any I have seen in England. In the moors in the north the hills and mountains are all covered with heath, like the Irish bogs, but they are of various soils, gravel, shingle, moor, etc., and boggy only in spots, but the Irish bog hills are all pure bog to a great depth without the least variation of soil; and the bog being of a hilly form, is a proof that it is a growing vegetable mass, and not owing merely to stagnant water. Sir Laurence Dundass is the principal proprietor of this.

Reached Ballymoat in the evening, the residence of the Hon. Mr. Fitzmaurice, where I expected great pleasure in viewing a manufactory, of which I heard much since I came to Ireland. He was so kind as to give me the following account of it in the most liberal manner:—

"Twenty years ago the late Lord Shelburne came to Ballymoat, a wild uncultivated region without industry or civility, and the people all Roman Catholics, without an atom of a manufacture, not even spinning. In order to change this state of things, his lordship contracted with people in the north to bring Protestant weavers and establish a manufactory, as the only means of making the change he wished. This was done, but falling into the hands of rascals he lost £5,000 by the business, with only seventeen Protestant families and twenty-six or twenty-seven looms established for it. Upon his death Lady Shelburne wished to carry his scheme into execution, and to do it gave much encouragement to Mr. Wakefield, the great Irish factor in London, by granting advantageous leases under the contract of building and colonising by weavers from the north, and carrying on the manufactory. He found about twenty looms working upon their own account, and made a considerable progress in this for five years, raising several buildings, cottages for the weavers, and was going on as well as the variety of his business would admit, employing sixty looms. He then died, when a stand was made to all the works for a year, in which everything went much to ruin. Lady Shelburne then employed a new manager to carry on the manufacture upon his own account, giving him very profitable grants of lands to encourage him to do it with spirit. He continued for five years, employing sixty looms also, but his circumstances failing, a fresh stop was put to the work.

"Then it was that Mr. Fitzmaurice, in the year 1774, determined to exert himself in pushing on a manufactory which promised to be of such essential service to the whole country. To do this with effect, he saw that it was necessary to take it entirely into his own hands. He could lend money to the manager to enable him to go on, but that would be at best hazardous, and could never do it in the complete manner in which he wished to establish it. In this period of consideration, Mr. Fitzmaurice was advised by his friends never to engage in so complex a business as a manufacture, in which he must of necessity become a merchant, also engage in all the hazard, irksomeness, etc., of commerce, so totally different from his birth, education, ideas, and pursuits; but tired with the inactivity of common life, he determined not only to turn manufacturer, but to carry on the business in the most spirited and vigorous manner that was possible. In the first place he took every means of making himself a complete master of the business; he went through various manufactures, inquired into the minutiæ, and took every measure to know it to the bottom. This he did so repeatedly and with such attention in the whole progress, from spinning to bleaching and selling, that he became as thorough a master of it as an experienced manager; he has wove linen, and done every part of the business with his own hands. As he determined to have the works complete, he took Mr. Stansfield the engineer, so well known for his improved saw-mills, into his pay. He sent him over to Ballymoat in the winter of 1774, in order to erect the machinery of a bleach mill upon the very best construction; he went to all the great mills in the north of Ireland to inspect them, to remark their deficiencies, that they might be improved in the mills he intended to erect. This knowledge being gained, the work was begun, and as water was necessary, a great basin was formed by a dam across a valley, by which means thirty-four acres were floated, to serve as a reservoir for dry seasons, to secure plenty at all times."

August 30. Rode to Rosshill, four miles off, a headland that projects into the Bay of Newport, from which there is a most beautiful view of the bay on both sides; I counted thirty islands very distinctly, all of them cultivated under corn and potatoes, or pastured by cattle. At a distance Clare rises in a very bold and picturesque style; on the left Crow Patrick, and to the right other mountains. It is a view that wants nothing but wood.

September 5. To Drumoland, the seat of Sir Lucius O'Brien, in the county of Clare, a gentleman who had been repeatedly assiduous to procure me every sort of information. I should remark, as I have now left Galway, that that county, from entering it in the road to Tuam till leaving it to-day, has been, upon the whole, inferior to most of the parts I have travelled in Ireland in point of beauty: there are not mountains of a magnitude to make the view striking. It is perfectly free from woods, and even trees, except about gentlemen's houses, nor has it a variety in its face. I do not, however, speak without exception; I passed some tracts which are cheerful. Drumoland has a pleasing variety of grounds about the house; it stands on a hill gently rising from a lake of twenty-four acres, in the middle of a noble wood of oak, ash, poplar, etc.; three beautiful hills rise above, over which the plantations spread in a varied manner; and these hills command very fine views of the great rivers Fergus and Shannon at their junction, being each of them a league wide.

There is a view of the Shannon from Limerick to Foynes Island, which is thirty miles, with all its bays, bends, islands, and fertile shores. It is from one to three miles broad, a most noble river, deserving regal navies for its ornament, or, what are better, fleets of merchantmen, the cheerful signs of far-extended commerce, instead of a few miserable fishing-boats, the only canvas that swelled upon the scene; but the want of commerce in her ports is the misfortune not the fault of Ireland—thanks for the deficiency to that illiberal spirit of trading jealousy, which has at times actuated and disgraced so many nations. The prospect has a noble outline in the bold mountains of Tipperary, Cork, Limerick, and Kerry. The whole view magnificent.

At the foot of this hill is the castle of Bunratty, a very large edifice, the seat of the O'Briens, princes of Thomond; it stands on the bank of a river, which falls into the Shannon near it. About this castle and that of Rosmanagher the land is the best in the county of Clare; it is worth £1 13s. an acre, and fats a bullock per acre in summer, besides winter feed.

To Limerick, through a cheerful country, on the banks of the river, in a vale surrounded by distant mountains. That city is very finely situated, partly on an island formed by the Shannon. The new part, called Newtown Pery, from Mr. Pery the speaker, who owns a considerable part of the city, and represents it in Parliament, is well built. The houses are new ones, of brick, large, and in right lines. There is a communication with the rest of the town by a handsome bridge of three large arches erected at Mr. Pery's expense. Here are docks, quays, and a custom-house, which is a good building, faces the river, and on the opposite banks is a large quadrangular one, the house of industry. This part of Limerick is very cheerful and agreeable, and carries all the marks of a flourishing place.

The exports of this port are beef, pork, butter, hides, and rape-seed. The imports are rum, sugar, timber, tobacco, wines, coals, bark, salt, etc. The customs and excise, about sixteen years ago, amounted to £16,000, at present £32,000, and rather more four or five years ago.

Revenue of the Port of Limerick. Year ending

Price of Provisions.

Land sells at twenty years' purchase. Rents were at the highest in 1765; fell since, but in four years have fallen 8s. to 10s. an acre about Limerick. They are at a stand at present, owing to the high price of provisions from pasture. The number of people in Limerick is computed at thirty-two thousand; it is exceedingly populous for the size, the chief street quite crowded; many sedan chairs in town, and some hackney chaises. Assemblies the year round, in a new assembly-house built for the purpose, and plays and concerts common.

Upon the whole, Limerick must be a very gay place, but when the usual number of troops are in town much more so. To show the general expenses of living, I was told of a person's keeping a carriage, four horses, three men, three maids, a good table, a wife, three children, and a nurse, and all for £500 a year:

A barrel of beef or pork, 200lb. weight. Vessels of 400 tons can come up with spring tides, which rise fourteen feet.

September 9. To Castle Oliver; various country, not so rich to appearance as the Caucasus, being fed bare; much hilly sheep walk, and for a considerable way a full third of it potatoes and corn: no sign of depopulation. Just before I got to the hills a field of ragwort (senesio jacobœa) buried the cows. The first hill of Castle Oliver interesting. After rising a mountain so high that no one could think of any house, you come in view of a vale, quite filled with fine woods, fields margined with trees, and hedge plantations climbing up the mountains. Having engaged myself to Mr. Oliver, to return from Killarney by his house, as he was confined to Limerick by the assizes, I shall omit saying anything of it at present.

September 16. To Cove by water, from Mr. Trent's quay. The view of Lota is charming; a fine rising lawn from the water, with noble spreading woods reaching on each side; the house a very pleasing front, with lawn shooting into the woods. The river forms a creek between two hills, one Lota, the other opening to another hill of inclosures well wooded. As the boat leaves the shore nothing can be finer than the view behind us; the back woods of Lota, the house and lawn, and the high bold inclosures towards Cork, form the finest shore imaginable, leading to Cork, the city appearing in full view, Dunkettle wooded inclosures, a fine sweep of hill, joining Mr. Hoare's at Factory Hill, whose woods have a beautiful effect. Dunkettle House almost lost in a wood. As we advance, the woods of Lota and Dunkettle unite in one fine mass. The sheet of water, the rising lawns, the house in the most beautiful situation imaginable, with more woods above it than lawns below it, the west shore of Loch Mahon, a very fine rising hill cut into inclosures but without wood, land-locked on every side with high lands, scattered with inclosures, woods, seats, etc., with every cheerful circumstance of lively commerce, have altogether a great effect. Advancing to Passage the shores are various, and the scenery enlivened by fourscore sail of large ships; the little port of Passage at the water's edge, with the hills rising boldly above it. The channel narrows between the great island and the hills of Passage. The shores bold, and the ships scattered about them, with the inclosures hanging behind the masts and yards picturesque. Passing the straits a new basin of the harbour opens, surrounded with high lands. Monkstown Castle on the hill to the right, and the grounds of Ballybricken, a beautiful intermixed scene of wood and lawn. The high shore of the harbour's mouth opens gradually. The whole scene is land-locked. The first view of Haulbowline Island and Spike Island, high rocky lands, with the channel opening to Cove, where are a fleet of ships at anchor, and Rostellan, Lord Inchiquin's house, backed with hills, a scenery that wants nothing but the accompaniment of wood. The view of Ballybricken changes; it now appears to be unfortunately cut into right lines. Arrived at the ship at Cove; in the evening returned, leaving Mr. Jefferys and family on board for a voyage to Havre, in their way to Paris.

Dunkettle is one of the most beautiful places I have seen in Ireland. It is a hill of some hundred acres broken into a great variety of ground by gentle declivities, with everywhere an undulating outline and the whole varied by a considerable quantity of wood, which in some places is thick enough to take the appearance of close groves, in others spreads into scattered thickets and a variety of single groups. This hill, or rather cluster of hills, is surrounded on one side by a reach of Cork Harbour, over which it looks in the most advantageous manner; and on the other by an irriguous vale, through which flows the river Glanmire; the opposite shore of that river has every variety that can unite to form pleasing landscapes for the views from Dunkettle grounds; in some places narrow glens, the bottoms of which are quite filled with water, and the steep banks covered with thick woods that spread a deep shade; in others the vale opens to form the site of a pretty cheerful village, overhung by hill and wood: here the shore rises gradually into large inclosures, which spread over the hills, stretching beyond each other; and there the vale melts again into a milder variety of fields. A hill thus situated, and consisting in itself of so much variety of surface, must necessarily command many pleasing views. To enjoy these to the better advantage, Mr. Trent (than whom no one has a better taste, both to discover and describe the beauties of natural scenes) is making a walk around the whole, which is to bend to the inequalities of the ground, so as to take the principal points in view. The whole is so beautiful, that if I were to make the regular detour, the description might be too minute; but there are some points which gave me so much pleasure that I know not how to avoid recommending to others that travel this way to taste the same satisfaction. From the upper part of the orchard you look down a part of the river, where it opens into a regular basin, one corner stretching up to Cork, lost behind the hill of Lota, the lawn of which breaks on the swelling hills among the woods; the house obscured, and therefore seeming a part of your home scene; the losing the river behind the beautiful projection of Lota is more pleasing than can be expressed. The other reach, leading to the harbour's mouth, is half hidden by the trees, which margin the foot of the hill on which you stand; in front a noble range of cultivated hills, the inclosures broken by slight spots of wood, and prettily varied with houses, without being so crowded as to take off the rural effect. The scene is not only beautiful in those common circumstances which form a landscape, but is alive with the cheerfulness of ships and boats perpetually moving. Upon the whole, it is one of the most luxuriant prospects I have anywhere seen. Leaving the orchard, pass on the brow of a hill which forms the bank of the river of Glanmire, commanding the opposite woods of Lota in all their beauty. Rise to the top of the high hill which joins the deer park, and exhibits a scene equally extensive and beautiful; you look down on a vale which winds almost around at your feet, finishing to the left in Cork river, which here takes the appearance of a lake, bounded by wood and hills, and sunk in the bottom of a vale, in a style which painting cannot imitate; the opposite hills of Lota, wood, and lawn, seem formed as objects for this point of view: at your feet a hill rises out of the vale, with higher ones around it, the margins scattered wood; to the right, towards Riverstown, a vale; the whole backed by cultivated hills to Kallahan's field. Milder scenes follow: a bird's-eye view of a small vale sunk at your feet, through which the river flows; a bridge of several arches unites two parts of a beautiful village, the meadow grounds of which rise gently, a varied surface of wood and lawn, to the hills of Riverstown, the whole surrounded by delicious sweeps of cultivated hills. To the left a wooded glen rising from the vale to the horizon, the scenery sequestered, but pleasing; the oak wood which hangs on the deer-park hills, an addition. Down to the brow of the hill, where it hangs over the river, a picturesque interesting spot. The inclosures of the opposite bank hang beautifully to the eye, and the wooded glen winds up the hill. Returning to the house I was conducted to the hill, where the grounds slope off to the river of Cork, which opens to view in noble reaches of a magnitude that fills the eye and the imagination; a whole country of a character truly magnificent, and behind the winding vale which leads between a series of hills to Glanmire.

Pictures at Dunkettle.

A St. Michael, etc., the subject confused, by Michael Angelo. A St. Francis on wood, a large original of Guido. A St. Cecilia, original of Romanelli. An Assumption of the Virgin, by L. Carracci. A Quaker's meeting, of above fifty figures, by Egbert Hemskerk. A sea view and rock piece, by Vernet. A small flagellation, by Sebastian del Piombo. A Madonna and Child, small, by Rubens. The Crucifixion, many figures in miniature, excellent, though the master is unknown. An excellent copy of the famous Danæ of Titian, at Monte Cavallo, near Naples, by Cioffi of Naples. Another of the Venus of Titian, at the Tribuna in Florence. Another of Venus blinding Cupid, by Titian, at the Palazzo Borghese in Rome. Another of great merit of the Madonna della Sedia of Raphael, at the Palazzo Pitti in Florence, by Stirn, a German, lately at Rome. Another of a Holy Family, from Raphael, of which there are said to be three originals, one at the king's palace in Naples, one in the Palais Royal in Paris, and the third in the collection of Lord Exeter, lately purchased at Rome. A portrait of Sir Patrick Trent, by Sir P. Lely. An excellent portrait of a person unknown, by Dahl.

September 17. To Castlemartyr, the seat of the Earl of Shannon, one of the most distinguished improvers in Ireland; in whom I found the most earnest desire to give me every species of information, with a knowledge and ability which enabled him to do it most effectually. Passed through Middleton, a well-built place, which belongs to the noble lord to whom it gives title. Castlemartyr is an old house, but much added to by the present earl; he has built, besides other rooms, a dining one thirty-two feet long by twenty-two broad, and a drawing one, the best rooms I have seen in Ireland, a double cube of twenty-five feet, being fifty long, twenty-five broad, and twenty-five high. The grounds about the house are very well laid out; much wood well grown, considerable lawns, a river made to wind through them in a beautiful manner, an old castle so perfectly covered with ivy as to be a picturesque object. A winding walk leads for a considerable distance along the banks of this river, and presents several pleasing landscapes.

From Rostellan to Lota, the seat of Frederick Rogers, Esq. I had before seen it in the highest perfection from the water going from Dunkettle to Cove, and from the grounds of Dunkettle. Mrs. Rogers was so obliging as to show me the back grounds, which are admirably wooded, and of a fine varied surface.

Got to Cork in the evening, and waited on the Dean, who received me with the most flattering attention. Cork is one of the most populous places I have ever been in; it was market-day, and I could scarce drive through the streets, they were so amazingly thronged: on the other days the number is very great. I should suppose it must resemble a Dutch town, for there are many canals in the streets, with quays before the houses. The best built part is Morrison's Island, which promises well; the old part of the town is very close and dirty. As to its commerce, the following particulars I owe to Robert Gordon, Esq., the surveyor-general:

Average of Nineteen Years' Export, ending March 24, 1773.

Average prices of the nineteen years on the custom books. All exports on those books are rated at the value of the reign of Charles II.; but the imports have always 10 per cent. on the sworn price added to them. Seventy to eighty sail of ships belong to Cork. Average of ships that entered that port in those nineteen years, eight hundred and seventy-two per annum. The number of people at Cork mustered by the clergy by hearth-money, and by the number of houses, payments to minister, average of the three, sixty-seven thousand souls, if taken before the 1st of September, after that twenty thousand increased. There are seven hundred coopers in the town. Barrels all of oak or beech, all from America: the latter for herrings, now from Gottenburg and Norway. The excise of Cork now no more than in Charles the Second's reign. Ridiculous!

Bullocks, 16,000 head, 32,000 barrels; 41,000 hogs, 20,000 barrels. Butter, 22,000 firkins of half a hundredweight each, both increase this year, the whole being

240,000 firkins of butter,

Export of woollen yarn from Cork, £300,000 a year in the Irish market. No wool smuggled, or at least very little. The wool comes to Cork, etc., and is delivered out to combers, who make it into balls. These balls are bought up by the French agents at a vast price, and exported; but even this does not amount to £40,000 a year.

Prices.

Beef, 21s. per cwt., never so high by 2s. 6d.; pork, 30s., never higher than 18s. 6d., owing to the army demand. Slaughter dung, 8d. for a horse load. Country labourer, 6d.; about town, 10d. Milk, seven pints a penny. Coals, 3s. 8d. to 5s. a barrel, six of which make a ton. Eggs, four a penny.

Cork labourers. Cellar ones, twenty thousand; have 1s. 1d. a day, and as much bread, beef, and beer as they can eat and drink, and seven pounds of offals a week for their families. Rent for their house, 40s. Masons' and carpenters' labourers, 10d. a day. Sailors now £3 a month and provisions: before the American war, 28s. Porters and coal-heavers paid by the great. State of the poor people in general incomparably better off than they were twenty years ago. There are imported eighteen thousand barrels annually of Scotch herrings, at 18s. a barrel. The salt for the beef trade comes from Lisbon, St. Ube's, etc. The salt for the fish trade from Rochelle. For butter English and Irish.

Particulars of the woollen fabrics of the county of Cork received from a manufacturer. The woollen trade, serges and camlets, ratteens, friezes, druggets, and narrow cloths, the last they make to 10s. and 12s. a yard; if they might export to 8s. they are very clear that they could get a great trade for the woollen manufactures of Cork. The wool comes from Galway and Roscommon, combed here by combers, who earn 8s. to 10s. a week, into balls of twenty-four ounces, which is spun into worsteds of twelve skeins to the ball, and exported to Yarmouth for Norwich; the export price, £30 a pack to £33, never before so high; average of them, £26 to £30. Some they work up at home into serges, stuffs, and camlets; the serges at 12d. a yard, thirty-four inches wide; the stuffs sixteen inches, at 18d., the camlets at 9½d. to 13d.; the spinners at 9d. a ball, one in a week; or a ball and half 12d. a week, and attend the family besides; this is done most in Waterford and Kerry, particularly near Killarney; the weavers earn 1s. a day on an average. Full three-fourths of the wool is exported in yarn, and only one-fourth worth worked up. Half the wool of Ireland is combed in the county of Cork.

A very great manufacture of ratteens at Carrick-on-Suir; the bay worsted is for serges, shalloons, etc. Woollen yarn for coarse cloths, which latter have been lost for some years, owing to the high price of wool. The bay export has declined since 1770, which declension is owing to the high price of wool.

No wool smuggled, not even from Kerry; not a sloop's cargo in twenty years, the price too high; the declension has been considerable. For every eighty-six packs that are exported, a licence from the Lord Lieutenant, for which £20 is paid.

From the Act of the last sessions of Great Britain for exporting woollen goods for the troops in the pay of Ireland, Mr. Abraham Lane, of Cork, established a new manufacture of army clothing for that purpose, which is the first at Cork, and pays £40 a week in labour only. Upon the whole there has been no increase of woollen manufacture within twenty years. Is clearly of opinion that many fabrics might be worked up here much cheaper than in France, of cloths that the French have beat the English out of; these are, particularly, broadcloths of one yard and half yard wide, from 3s. to 6s. 6d. a yard for the Levant trade. Friezes which are now supplied from Carcassone in Languedoc. Friezes, of twenty-four to twenty-seven inches, at 10d. to 13d. a yard. Flannels, twenty-seven to thirty-six, from 7d. to 14d. Serges of twenty-seven to thirty-six inches, at 7d. to 12d. a yard; these would work up the coarse wool. At Ballynasloe Fair, in July, £200,000 a year bought in wool. There is a manufactory of knit-stocking by the common women about Cork, for eight or ten miles around; the yarn from 12d. to 18d. a pair, and the worsted from 16d. to 20d., and earn from 12d. to 18d. a week. Besides their own consumption, great quantities are sent to the north of Ireland.

All the weavers in the country are confined to towns, have no land, but small gardens. Bandle, or narrow linen, for home consumption, is made in the western part of the county. Generally speaking, the circumstances of all the manufacturing poor are better than they were twenty years ago. The manufactures have not declined, though the exportation has, owing to the increased home consumptions. Bandon was once the seat of the stuff, camlet, and shag manufacture, but has in seven years declined above three-fourths. Have changed it for the manufacture of coarse green linens, for the London market, from 6d. to 9d. a yard, twenty-seven inches wide; but the number of manufactures in general much lessened.

Rode to the mouth of Cork Harbour; the grounds about it are all fine, bold, and varied, but so bare of trees, that there is not a single view but what pains one in the want of wood. Rents of the tract south of the river Caragoline, from 5s. to 30s.; average, 10s. Not one man in five has a cow, but generally from one to four acres, upon which they have potatoes, and five or six sheep, which they milk, and spin their wool. Labour 5d. in winter, 6d. in summer; many of them for three months in the year live on potatoes and water, the rest of it they have a good deal of fish. But it is remarked, at Kinsale, that when sprats are most plentiful, diseases are most common. Rent for a mere cabin, 10s. Much paring and burning; paring twenty-eight men a day, sow wheat on it and then potatoes; get great crops. The soil a sharp, stony land; no limestone south of the above river. Manure for potatoes, with sea-weed, for 26s., which gives good crops, but lasts only one year. Sea-sand much used; no shells in it. Farms rise to two or three hundred acres, but are hired in partnership.

Before I quit the environs of Cork, I must remark that the country on the harbour I think preferable, in many respects, for a residence, to anything I have seen in Ireland. First, it is the most southerly part of the kingdom. Second, there are very great beauties of prospect. Third, by much the most animated, busy scene of shipping in all Ireland, and consequently, fourth, a ready price for every product. Fifth, great plenty of excellent fish and wild fowl. Sixth, the neighbourhood of a great city for objects of convenience.

September 25. Took the road to Nedeen, through the wildest region of mountains that I remember to have seen; it is a dreary but an interesting road. The various horrid, grotesque, and unusual forms in which the mountains rise and the rocks bulge; the immense height of some distant heads, which rear above all the nearer scenes, the torrents roaring in the vales, and breaking down the mountain sides, with here and there a wretched cabin, and a spot of culture yielding surprise to find human beings the inhabitants of such a scene of wildness, altogether keep the traveller's mind in an agitation and suspense. These rocks and mountains are many of them no otherwise improvable than by planting, for which, however, they are exceedingly well adapted.

Sir John Colthurst was so obliging as to send half a dozen labourers with me, to help my chaise up a mountain side, of which he gave a formidable account: in truth it deserved it. The road leads directly against a mountain ridge, and those who made it were so incredibly stupid, that they kept the straight line up the hill, instead of turning aside to the right to wind around a projection of it. The path of the road is worn by torrents into a channel, which is blocked up in places by huge fragments, so that it would be a horrid road on a level; but on a hill so steep, that the best path would be difficult to ascend—it may be supposed terrible: the labourers, two passing strangers, and my servant, could with difficulty get the chaise up. It is much to be regretted that the direction of the road is not changed, as all the rest from Cork to Nedeen is good enough. For a few miles towards the latter place the country is flat on the river Kenmare, much of it good, and under grass or corn. Passed Mr. Orpine's at Ardtilly, and another of the same name at Killowen.

Nedeen is a little town, very well situated, on the noble river Kenmare, where ships of one hundred and fifty tons may come up; there are but three or four good houses. Lord Shelburne, to whom the place belongs, has built one for his agent. There is a vale of good land, which is here from a mile and a half to a mile broad; and to the north and south, great ridges of mountains said to be full of mines.

At Nedeen, Lord Shelburne had taken care to have me well informed by his people in that country, which belongs for the greatest part to himself, he has above one hundred and fifty thousand Irish acres in Kerry; the greatest part of the barony of Glanrought belongs to him, most of Dunkerron and Ivragh. The country is all a region of mountains, inclosed by a vale of flat land on the river; the mountains to the south come to the water's edge, with but few variations, the principal of which is Ardee, a farm of Lord Shelburne's to the north of the river, the flat land is one-half to three-quarters of a mile broad. The mountains to the south reach to Bear-haven, and those to the north to Dingle Bay; the soil is extremely various; to the south of the river all are sandstones, and the hills loam, stone, gravel, and bog. To the north there is a slip of limestone land, from Kilgarvon to Cabbina-cush, that is six miles east of Nedeen, and three to the west, but is not more than a quarter of a mile broad, the rest, including the mountains, all sandstone. As to its rents, it is very difficult to tell what they are; for land is let by the plough-land and gineve, twelve gineves to the plough-land; but the latter denomination is not of any particular quantity, for no two plough-lands are the same. The size of farms is various, from forty acres to one thousand; less quantities go with cabins, and some farms are taken by labourers in partnership.

Soon entered the wildest and most romantic country I had anywhere seen; a region of steep rocks and mountains which continued for nine or ten miles, till I came in view of Mucruss. There is something magnificently wild in this stupendous scenery, formed to impress the mind with a certain species of terror. All this tract has a rude and savage air, but parts of it are strikingly interesting; the mountains are bare and rocky, and of a great magnitude; the vales are rocky glens, where a mountain stream tumbles along the roughest bed imaginable, and receives many torrents, pouring from clefts, half overhung with shrubby wood; some of these streams are seen, and the roar of others heard, but hid by vast masses of rock. Immense fragments, torn from the precipices by storms and torrents, are tumbled in the wildest confusion, and seem to hang rather than rest upon projecting precipices. Upon some of these fragments of rock, perfectly detached from the soil, except by the side on which they lie, are beds of black turf, with luxuriant crops of heath, etc., which appeared very curious to me, having nowhere seen the like; and I observed very high in the mountains—much higher than any cultivation is at present, on the right hand—flat and cleared spaces of good grass among the ridges of rock, which had probably been cultivated, and proved that these mountains were not incapable from climate of being applied to useful purposes.

From one of these heights I looked forward to the Lake of Killarney at a considerable distance, and backward to the river Kenmare; came in view of a small part of the upper lake, spotted with several islands, and surrounded by the most tremendous mountains that can be imagined, of an aspect savage and dreadful. From this scene of wild magnificence, I broke at once upon all the glories of Killarney; from an elevated point of view I looked down on a considerable part of the lake, which gave me a specimen of what I might expect. The water you command (which, however, is only a part of the lake) appears a basin of two or three miles round; to the left it is inclosed by the mountains you have passed, particularly by the Turk, whose outline is uncommonly noble, and joins a range of others, that form the most magnificent shore in the world: on the other side is a rising scenery of cultivated hills, and Lord Kenmare's park and woods; the end of the lake at your feet is formed by the root of Mangerton, on whose side the road leads. From hence I looked down on a pretty range of inclosures on the lake, and the woods and lawns of Mucruss, forming a large promontory of thick wood, shooting far into the lake. The most active fancy can sketch nothing in addition. Islands of wood beyond seem to join it, and reaches of the lake, breaking partly between, give the most lively intermixture of water; six or seven isles and islets form an accompaniment: some are rocky, but with a slight vegetation, others contain groups of trees, and the whole thrown into forms, which would furnish new ideas to a painter. Farther is a chain of wooded islands, which also appear to join the mainland, with an offspring of lesser ones scattered around.

Arrived at Mr. Herbert's at Mucruss, to whose friendly attention I owed my succeeding pleasure. There have been so many descriptions of Killarney written by gentlemen who have resided some time there, and seen it at every season, that for a passing traveller to attempt the like would be in vain; for this reason I shall give the mere journal of the remarks I made on the spot, in the order I viewed the lake.

September 27. Walked into Mr. Herbert's beautiful grounds, to Oroch's Hill, in the lawn that he has cleared from that profusion of stones which lie under the wall; the scene which this point commands is truly delicious; the house is on the edge of the lawn, by a wood which covers the whole peninsula, fringes the slope at your feet, and forms a beautiful shore to the lake. Tomys and Glená are vast mountainous masses of incredible magnificence, the outline soft and easy in its swells, whereas those above the eagle's nest are of so broken and abrupt an outline, that nothing can be imagined more savage, an aspect horrid and sublime, that gives all the impressions to be wished to astonish rather than please the mind. The Turk exhibits noble features, and Mangerton's huge body rises above the whole. The cultivated tracts towards Killarney form a shore in contrast to the terrific scenes I have just mentioned; the distant boundary of the lake, a vast ridge of distant blue mountains towards Dingle. From hence entered the garden, and viewed Mucruss Abbey, one of the most interesting scenes I ever saw; it is the ruin of a considerable abbey, built in Henry VI.'s time, and so entire, that if it were more so, though the building would be more perfect, the ruin would be less pleasing; it is half obscured in the shade of some venerable ash trees; ivy has given the picturesque circumstance, which that plant alone can confer, while the broken walls and ruined turrets throw over it

heaps of skulls and bones scattered about, with nettles, briars, and weeds sprouting in tufts from the loose stones, all unite to raise those melancholy impressions, which are the merit of such scenes, and which can scarcely anywhere be felt more completely. The cloisters form a dismal area, in the centre of which grows the most prodigious yew-tree I ever beheld, in one great stem, two feet diameter, and fourteen feet high, from whence a vast head of branches spreads on every side, so as to perform a perfect canopy to the whole space. I looked for its fit inhabitant; it is a spot where

This ruin is in the true style in which all such buildings should appear; there is not an intruding circumstance, the hand of dress has not touched it, melancholy is the impression which such scenes should kindle, and it is here raised most powerfully.

From the abbey we passed to the terrace, a natural one of grass, on the very shore of the lake; it is irregular and winding; a wall of rocks broken into fantastic forms by the waves: on the other side a wood, consisting of all sorts of plants, which the climate can protect, and through which a variety of walks are traced. The view from this terrace consists of many parts of various characters, but in their different styles complete; the lake opens a spreading sheet of water, spotted by rocks and islands, all but one or two wooded; the outlines of them are sharp and distinct; nothing can be more smiling than this scene, soft and mild, a perfect contrast of beauty to the sublimity of the mountains which form the shore: these rise in an outline, so varied, and at the same time so magnificent, that nothing greater can be imagined; Tomys and Glená exhibit an immensity in point of magnitude, but from a large hanging wood on the slope, and from the smoothness of the general surface, it has nothing savage, whereas the mountains above and near the eagle's nest are of the most broken outlines; the declivities are bulging rocks, of immense size, which seem to impend in horrid forms over the lake, and where an opening among them is caught, others of the same rude character rear their threatening heads. From different parts of the terrace these scenes are viewed in numberless varieties.

Returned to breakfast, and pursued Mr. Herbert's new road, which he has traced through the peninsula to Dynis Island, three miles in length; and it is carried in so judicious a manner through a great variety of ground, rocky woods, lawns, etc., that nothing can be more pleasing; it passes through a remarkable scene of rocks, which are covered with woods. From thence to the marble quarry, which Mr. Herbert is working, and where he gains variety of marbles, green, red, white, and brown, prettily veined; the quarry is a shore of rocks, which surround a bay of the lake, and forms a scene consisting of but few parts, but those strongly marked; the rocks are bold, and broken into slight caverns; they are fringed with scattered trees, and from many parts of them wood shoots in that romantic manner so common at Killarney. Full in front Turk Mountain rises with the proudest outline, in that abrupt magnificence which fills up the whole space before one, and closes the scene.

The road leads by a place where copper-mines were worked; many shafts appear; as much ore was raised as sold for twenty-five thousand pounds, but the works were laid aside, more from ignorance in the workmen than any defects in the mine.

Came to the opening on the great lake, which appears to advantage here, the town of Killarney on the north-east shore. Look full on the mountain Glená, which rises in very bold manner, the hanging woods spread half way, and are of great extent, and uncommonly beautiful. Two very pleasing scenes succeed; that to the left is a small bay, hemmed in by a neck of land in front; the immediate shore rocks, which are in a picturesque style, and crowned entirely with arbutus, and other wood; a pretty retired scene, where a variety of objects give no fatigue to the eye. The other is an admirable mixture of the beautiful and sublime: a bare rock of an almost regular figure projects from a headland into the lake, which, with much wood and highland, forms one side of the scene; the other is wood from a rising ground only; the lake open between, in a sheet of no great extent, but in front is the hanging wood of Glená, which appears in full glory.

Mr. Herbert has built a handsome Gothic bridge, to unite the peninsula to the island of Brickeen, through the arch of which the waters of the north and south lake flow. It is a span of twenty-seven feet, and seventeen high, and over it the road leads to that island. From thence to Brickeen nearly finished, and it is to be thrown across a bottom into Dynis.

Returned by the northern path through a thick wood for some distance, and caught a very agreeable view of Ash Island, seen through an opening, inclosed on both sides with wood. Pursued the way from these grounds to Keelbeg, and viewed the bay of the Devil's Island, which is a beautiful one, inclosed by a shore, to the right of very noble rocks in ledges and other forms, crowned in a striking manner with wood; a little rocky islet rises in front; to the left the water opens, and Turk Mountain rises with that proud superiority which attends him in all these scenes.

The view of the promontory of Dindog, near this place, closes this part of the lake, and is indeed singularly beautiful. It is a large rock, which shoots far into the water, of a height sufficient to be interesting, in full relief, fringed with a scanty vegetation; the shore on which you stand bending to the right, as if to meet that rock, presents a circular shade of dark wood: Turk still the background, in a character of great sublimity, and Mangerton's loftier summit, but less interesting outline, a part of the scenery. These views, with others of less moment, are connected by a succession of lawns breaking among the wood, pleasing the eye with lively verdure, and relieving it from the fatigue of the stupendous mountain scenes.

September 28. Took boat on the lake, from the promontory of Dindog before mentioned. I had been under a million of apprehensions that I should see no more of Killarney; for it blew a furious storm all night, and in the morning the bosom of the lake heaved with agitation, exhibiting few marks but those of anger. After breakfast it cleared up, the clouds dispersed by degrees, the waves subsided, the sun shone out in all its splendour; every scene was gay, and no ideas but pleasure possessed the breast. With these emotions sallied forth, nor did they disappoint us.

Rowed under the rocky shore of Dindog, which is romantic to a great degree. The base, by the beating of the waves, is worn into caverns, so that the heads of the rocks project considerably beyond the base, and hang over in a manner which makes every part of it interesting. Following the coast, open marble quarry bay, the shore great fragments of rock tumbled about in the wildest manner.

The island of rocks against the copper-mine shore a remarkable group. The shore near Casemilan is of a different nature; it is wood in some places, in unbroken masses down to the water's edge, in others divided from it by smaller tracts of rock. Come to a beautiful land-locked bay, surrounded by a woody shore, which, opening in places, shows other woods more retired. Tomys is here viewed in a unity of form, which gives it an air of great magnificence. Turk was obscured by the sun shining immediately above him, and, casting a stream of burning light on the water, displayed an effect to describe which the pencil of a Claude alone would be equal. Turn out of the bay, and gain a full view of the Eagle's Nest, the mountains above it, and Glená; they form a perfect contrast; the first are rugged, but Glená mild. Here the shore is a continued wood.

Pass the bridge, and cross to Dynis, an island Mr. Herbert has improved in the most agreeable manner, by cutting walks through it that command a variety of views. One of these paths on the banks of the channel to the upper lake is sketched with great taste; it is on one side walled with natural rocks, from clefts of which shoot a thousand fine arbutuses, that hang in a rich foliage of flowers and scarlet berries; a turf bench in a delicious spot; the scene close and sequestered, just enough to give every pleasing idea annexed to retirement.

Passing the bridge, by a rapid stream, came presently to the Eagle's Nest: having viewed this rock from places where it appears only a part of an object much greater than itself, I had conceived an idea that it did not deserve the applause given it, but upon coming near I was much surprised; the approach is wonderfully fine, the river leads directly to its foot, and does not give the turn till immediately under, by which means the view is much more grand than it could otherwise be; it is nearly perpendicular, and rises in such full majesty, with so bold an outline, and such projecting masses in its centre, that the magnificence of the object is complete. The lower part is covered with wood, and scattered trees climb almost to the top, which (if trees can be amiss in Ireland) rather weaken the impression raised by this noble rock. This part is a hanging wood, or an object whose character is perfect beauty; but the upper scene, the broken outline, rugged sides, and bulging masses, all are sublime, and so powerful, that sublimity is the general impression of the whole, by overpowering the idea of beauty raised by the wood. This immense height of the mountains of Killarney may be estimated by this rock; from any distant place that commands it, it appears the lowest crag of a vast chain, and of no account; but on a close approach it is found to command a very different respect.

Pass between the mountains called the Great Range, towards the upper lake. Here Turk, which has so long appeared with a figure perfectly interesting, is become, from a different position, an unmeaning lump. The rest of the mountains, as you pass, assume a varied appearance, and are of a prodigious magnitude. The scenery in this channel is great and wild in all its features; wood is very scarce; vast rocks seem tossed in confusion through the narrow vale, which is opened among the mountains for the river to pass. Its banks are rocks in a hundred forms; the mountain-sides are everywhere scattered with them. There is not a circumstance but is in unison with the wild grandeur of the scene.

Coleman's Eye, a narrow pass, opens a different scenery. Came to a region in which the beautiful and the great are mixed without offence. The islands are most of them thickly wooded. Oak Isle in particular rises on a pretty base, and is a most beautiful object: Macgillicuddy Reeks, with their broken points; Baum, with his perfect cone; the Purple Mountain, with his broad and more regular head; and Turk, having assumed a new and more interesting aspect, unite with the opposite hills, part of which have some wood left on them, to form a scene uncommonly striking. Here you look back on a very peculiar spot; it is a parcel of rocks which cross the lake, and form a gap that opens to distant water, the whole backed by Turk, in a style of the highest grandeur.

Come to Derry Currily, which is a great sweep of mountain, covered partly with wood, hanging in a very noble manner, but part cut down, much of it mangled, and the rest inhabited by coopers, boat-builders, carpenters, and turners, a sacrilegious tribe, who have turned the Dryads from their ancient habitations. The cascade here is a fine one; but passed quickly from hence to scenes unmixed with pain.

Row to the cluster of the Seven Islands, a little archipelago; they rise very boldly from the water upon rocky bases, and are crowned in the most beautiful manner with wood, among which are a number of arbutuses; the channels among them opening to new scenes, and the great amphitheatre of rock and mountain that surround them unite to form a noble view.

Into the river, at the very end of the lake, which winds towards Macgillicuddy Reeks in fanciful meanders.

Returned by a course somewhat different, through the Seven Islands, and back to the Eagle's Nest, viewing the scenes already mentioned in new positions. At that noble rock fired three cannon for the echo, which indeed is prodigious; the report does not consist of direct reverberations from one rock to another with a pause between, but has an exact resemblance to a peal of thunder rattling behind the rock, as if travelling the whole scenery we had viewed, and lost in the immensity of Macgillicuddy Reeks.

Returning through the bridge, turn to the left round Dynis Island, under the woods of Glená; open on the cultivated country beyond the town of Killarney, and come gradually in sight of Innisfallen and Ross Island.

Pass near to the wood of Glená, which here takes the appearance of one immense sweep hanging in the most beautiful manner imaginable, on the side of a vast mountain to a point, shooting into the great lake. A more glorious scene is not to be imagined. It is one deep mass of wood, composed of the richest shades perfectly dipping in the water, without rock or strand appearing, not a break in the whole. The eye passing upon the sheet of liquid silver some distance, to meet so entire a sweep of every tint that can compose one vast mass of green, hanging to such an extent as to fill not only the eye but the imagination, unites in the whole to form the most noble scene that is anywhere to be beheld.

Turn under the north shore of Mucruss; the lake here is one great expanse of water, bounded by the woods described, the islands of Innisfallen, Ross, etc., and the peninsula. The shore of Mucruss has a great variety; it is in some places rocky; huge masses tumbled from their base lie beneath, as in a chaos of ruin. Great caverns worn under them in a variety of strange forms; or else covered with woods of a variety of shades. Meet the point of Ardnagluggen (in English where the water dashes on the rocks) and come under Ornescope, a rocky headland of a most bold projection hanging many yards over its base, with an old weather-beaten yew growing from a little bracket of rock, from which the spot is called Ornescope, or yew broom.

Mucruss gardens presently open among the woods, and relieve the eye, almost fatigued with the immense objects upon which it has so long gazed; these softer scenes of lawn gently swelling among the shrubs and trees finished the second day.

September 29. Rode after breakfast to Mangerton Cascade and Drumarourk Hill, from which the view of Mucruss is uncommonly pleasing.

Pass the other hill, the view of which I described the 27th, and went to Colonel Huffy's monument, from whence the scene is different from the rest; the foreground is a gentle hill, intersected by hedges, forming several small lawns. There are some scattered trees and houses, with Mucruss Abbey half obscured by wood, the whole cheerful and backed by Turk. The lake is of a triangular form, Ross Island and Innisfallen its limits; the woods of Mucruss and the islands take a new position.

Returning, took a boat again towards Ross Isle, and as Mucruss retires from us, nothing can be more beautiful than the spots of lawn in the terrace opening in the wood; above it the green hills with clumps, and the whole finishing in the noble group of wood about the abbey, which here appears a deep shade, and so fine a finishing one, that not a tree should be touched. Rowed to the east point of Ross, which is well wooded; turn to the south coast. Doubling the point, the most beautiful shore of that island appears; it is the well-wooded environs of a bay, except a small opening to the castle; the woods are in deep shades, and rise on the regular slopes of a high range of rocky coast. The part in front of Filekilly point rises in the middle, and sinks towards each end. The woods of Tomys here appear uncommonly fine. Open Innisfallen, which is composed at this distance of the most various shades, within a broken outline, entirely different from the other islands, groups of different masses rising in irregular tufts, and joined by lower trees. No pencil could mix a happier assemblage. Land near a miserable room, where travellers dine. Of the isle of Innisfallen, it is paying no great compliment to say it is the most beautiful in the king's dominions, and perhaps in Europe. It contains twenty acres of land, and has every variety that the range of beauty, unmixed with the sublime, can give. The general feature is that of wood; the surface undulates into swelling hills, and sinks into little vales; the slopes are in every direction, the declivities die gently away, forming those slight inequalities which are the greatest beauty of dressed grounds. The little valleys let in views of the surrounding lake between the hills, while the swells break the regular outline of the water, and give to the whole an agreeable confusion. The wood has all the variety into which nature has thrown the surface; in some parts it is so thick as to appear impenetrable, and secludes all farther view; in others, it breaks into tufts of tall timber, under which cattle feed. Here they open, as if to offer to the spectator the view of the naked lawn; in others close, as if purposely to forbid a more prying examination. Trees of large size and commanding figure form in some places natural arches; the ivy mixing with the branches, and hanging across in festoons of foliage, while on one side the lake glitters among the trees, and on the other a thick gloom dwells in the recesses of the wood. The figure of the island renders one part a beautiful object to another; for the coast being broken and indented, forms bays surrounded either with rock or wood: slight promontories shoot into the lake, whose rocky edges are crowned with wood. These are the great features of Innisfallen; the slighter touches are full of beauties easily imagined by the reader. Every circumstance of the wood, the water, the rocks, and lawn, are characteristic, and have a beauty in the assemblage from mere disposition. I must, however, observe that this delicious retreat is not kept as one could wish.

Scenes that are great and commanding, from magnitude or wildness, should never be dressed; the rugged, and even the horrible, may add to the effect upon the mind: but in such as Innisfallen, a degree of dress, that is, cleanliness, is even necessary to beauty. I have spoken of lawn, but I should observe that expression indicates what it ought to be rather than what it is. It is very rich grass, poached by oxen and cows, the only inhabitants of the island. No spectator of taste but will regret the open grounds not being drained with hollow cuts; the ruggedness of the surface levelled, and the grass kept close shaven by many sheep instead of beasts. The bushes and briars, where they have encroached on what ought to be lawn, cleared away; some parts of the isle more opened; in a word no ornaments given, for the scene wants them not, but obstructions cleared, ruggedness smoothed, and the whole cleaned. This is what ought to be done; as to what might be made of the island, if its noble proprietor (Lord Kenmare) had an inclination, it admits of being converted into a terrestrial paradise; lawning with the intermixture of other shrubs and wood, and a little dress, would make it an example of what ornamented grounds might be, but which not one in a thousand is. Take the island, however, as it is, with its few imperfections, and where are we to find such another? What a delicious retreat! an emperor could not bestow such a one as Innisfallen; with a cottage, a few cows, and a swarm of poultry, is it possible that happiness should refuse to be a guest here?

Row to Ross Castle, in order to coast that island; there is nothing peculiarly striking in it; return the same way around Innisfallen. In this little voyage the shore of Ross is one of the most beautiful of the wooded ones in the lake; it seems to unite with Innisfallen, and projects into the water in thick woods one beyond another. In the middle of the channel a large rock, and from the other shore a little promontory of a few scattered trees; the whole scene pleasing.

The shore of Innisfallen has much variety, but in general it is woody, and of the beautiful character which predominates in that island. One bay, at taking leave of it, is exceedingly pretty; it is a semicircular one, and in the centre there is a projecting knoll of wood within a bay; this is uncommon, and has an agreeable effect.

The near approach to Tomys exhibits a sweep of wood, so great in extent, and so rich in foliage, that no person can see without admiring it. The mountainous part above is soon excluded by the approach; wood alone is seen, and that in such a noble range as to be greatly striking; it just hollows into a bay, and in the centre of it is a chasm in the wood; this is a bed of a considerable stream, which forms O'Sullivan's cascade, to which all strangers are conducted, as one of the principal beauties of Killarney. Landed to the right of it, and walked under the thick shade of the wood, over a rocky declivity, close to the torrent stream, which breaks impetuously from rock to rock, with a roar that kindles expectation. The picture in your fancy will not exceed the reality; a great stream bursts from the deep bosom of a wooded glen, hollowed into a retired recess of rocks and trees, itself a most pleasing and romantic spot, were there not a drop of water: the first fall is many feet perpendicularly over a rock; to the eye it immediately makes another, the basin into which it pours being concealed; from this basin it forces itself impetuously between two rocks. This second fall is also of a considerable height; but the lower one, the third, is the most considerable; it issues in the same manner from a basin hid from the point of view. These basins being large, there appears a space of several yards between each fall, which adds much to the picturesque scenery; the whole is within an arch of wood, that hangs over it; the quantity of water is so considerable, as to make an almost deafening noise, and uniting with the torrent below, where the fragments of rock are large and numerous, throw an air of grandeur over the whole. It is about seventy feet high. Coast from hence the woody shores of Tomys and Glená; they are upon the whole much the most beautiful ones I have anywhere seen; Glená woods having more oak, and some arbutuses, are the finer and deeper shades; Tomys has a great quantity of birch, whose foliage is not so luxuriant. The reader may figure to himself what these woods are, when he is informed that they fill an unbroken extent of six miles in length, and from half a mile to a mile and a half in breadth, all hanging on the sides of two vast mountains, and coming down with a full robe of rich luxuriance to the very water's edge. The acclivity of these hills is such, that every tree appears full to the eye. The variety of the ground is great; in some places great swells in the mountain-side, with corresponding hollows, present concave and convex masses; in others, considerable ridges of land and rock rise from the sweep, and offer to the astonished eye yet other varieties of shade. Smaller mountains rise regularly from the immense bosom of the larger, and hold forth their sylvan heads, backed by yet higher woods. To give all the varieties of this immense scenery of forest is impossible. Above the whole is a prodigious mass of mountain, of a gently swelling outline and soft appearance, varying as the sun or clouds change their position, but never becoming rugged or threatening to the eye.

The variations are best seen by rowing near the shore, when every stroke of the oar gives a new outline, and fresh tints to please the eye: but for one great impression, row about two miles from the shore of Glená; at that distance the inequalities in the surface are no longer seen, but the eye is filled with so immense a range of wood, crowned with a mountain in perfect unison with itself, that objects, whose character is that of beauty, are here, from their magnitude, truly magnificent, and attended with a most forcible expression.—Returned to Mucruss.

September 30. This morning I had dedicated to the ascent of Mangerton, but his head was so enshrouded in clouds, and the weather so bad, that I was forced to give up the scheme: Mr. Herbert has measured him with very accurate instruments, of which he has a great collection, and found his height eight hundred and thirty-five yards above the level of the sea. The Devil's Punch-bowl, from the description I had of it, must be the crater of an exhausted volcano: there are many signs of them about Killarney, particularly vast rocks on the sides of mountains, in streams, as if they had rolled from the top in one direction. Brown stone rocks are also sometimes found on lime-quarries, tossed thither perhaps in some vast eruption.

In my way from Killarney to Castle Island, rode into Lord Kenmare's park, from whence there is another beautiful view of the lake, different from many of the preceding; there is a broad margin of cultivated country at your feet, to lead the eye gradually in the lake, which exhibits her islands to this point more distinctly than to any other, and the backgrounds of the mountains of Glená and Tomys give a bold relief.

Upon the whole, Killarney, among the lakes that I have seen, can scarcely be said to have a rival. The extent of water in Loch Earne is much greater, the islands more numerous, and some scenes near Castle Caldwell of perhaps as great magnificence. The rocks at Keswick are more sublime, and other lakes may have circumstances in which they are superior; but when we consider the prodigious woods of Killarney, the immensity of the mountains, the uncommon beauty of the promontory of Mucruss and the Isle of Innisfallen, the character of the islands, the singular circumstance of the arbutus, and the uncommon echoes, it will appear, upon the whole, to be in reality superior to all comparison.

Before I quit it I have one other observation to make, which is relative to the want of accommodations and extravagant expense of strangers residing at Killarney. I speak it not at all feelingly, thanks to Mr. Herbert's hospitality, but from the accounts given me: the inns are miserable, and the lodgings little better. I am surprised somebody with a good capital does not procure a large well-built inn, to be erected on the immediate shore of the lake, in an agreeable situation, at a distance from the town; there are very few places where such a one would answer better; there ought to be numerous and good apartments. A large rendezvous-room for billiards, cards, dancing, music, etc., to which the company might resort when they chose it; an ordinary for those that like dining in public; boats of all sorts, nets for fishing, and as great a variety of amusements as could be collected, especially within doors; for the climate being very rainy, travellers wait with great impatience in a dirty common inn, which they would not do if they were in the midst of such accommodations as they meet with at an English spa. But above all, the prices of everything, from a room and a dinner to a barge and a band of music, to be reasonable, and hung up in every part of the house. The resort of strangers to Killarney would then be much increased, and their stay would be greatly prolonged; they would not view it post-haste, and fly away the first moment to avoid dirt and imposition. A man with a good capital and some ingenuity would, I think, make a fortune by fixing here upon such principles.

The state of the poor in the whole county of Kerry represented as exceedingly miserable, and owing to the conduct of men of property, who are apt to lay the blame on what they call land pirates, or men who offer the highest rent, and who, in order to pay this rent, must and do re-let all the cabin lands at an extravagant rise, which is assigning over all the cabins to be devoured by one farmer. The cottars on a farm cannot go from one to another, in order to find a good master, as in England; for all the country is in the same system, and no redress to be found. Such being the case, the farmers are enabled to charge the price of labour as low as they please, and rate the land as high as they like. This is an evil which oppresses them cruelly, and certainly has its origin in its landlords when they set their farms, setting all the cabins with them, instead of keeping them tenants to themselves. The oppression is, the farmer valuing the labour of the poor at fourpence or fivepence a day, and paying that in land rated much above its value. Owing to this the poor are depressed; they live upon potatoes and sour milk, and the poorest of them only salt and water to them, with now and then a herring. Their milk is bought; for very few keep cows, scarce any pigs, but a few poultry. Their circumstances are incomparably worse than they were twenty years ago; for they had all cows, but then they wore no linen: all now have a little flax. To these evils have been owing emigrations, which have been considerable.

To the west of Tralee are the Mahagree Islands, famous for their corn products; they are rock and sand, stocked with rabbits; near them a sandy tract, twelve miles long, and one mile broad, to the north, with the mountains to the south, famous for the best wheat in Kerry; all under the plough.

Arriving at Ardfert, Lord Crosby, whose politeness I have every reason to remember, was so obliging as to carry me by one of the finest strands I ever rode upon, to view the mouth of the Shannon at Ballengary, the site of an old fort. It is a vast rock, separated from the country by a chasm of prodigious depth, through which the waves drive. The rocks of the coast here are in the boldest style, and hollowed by the furious Atlantic waves into caverns in which they roar. It was a dead calm, yet the swell was so heavy, that the great waves rolled in and broke upon the rocks with such violence as to raise an immense foam, and give one an idea of what a storm would be; but fancy rarely falls short in her pictures. The view of the Shannon is exceedingly noble; it is eight miles over, the mouth formed by two headlands of very high and bold cliffs, and the reach of the river in view very extensive; it is an immense scenery: perhaps the noblest mouth of a river in Europe.

Ardfert is very near the sea, so near it that single trees or rows are cut in pieces with the wind, yet about Lord Glendour's house there are extensive plantations exceedingly flourishing, many fine ash and beech; about a beautiful Cistercian abbey, and a silver fir of forty-eight years' growth, of an immense height and size.

October 3. Left Ardfert, accompanying Lord Crosby to Listowel. Called in the way to view Lixnaw, the ancient seat of the Earls of Kerry, but deserted for ten years past, and now presents so melancholy a scene of desolation, that it shocked me to see it. Everything around lies in ruin, and the house itself is going fast off by thieving depredations of the neighbourhood. I was told a curious anecdote of this estate; which shows wonderfully the improvement of Ireland. The present Earl of Kerry's grandfather, Thomas, agreed to lease the whole estate for £1,500 a year to a Mr. Collis for ever, but the bargain went off upon a dispute whether the money should be paid at Cork or Dublin. Those very lands are now let at £20,000 a year. There is yet a good deal of wood, particularly a fine ash grove, planted by the present Earl of Shelburne's father.

Proceeded to Woodford, Robert Fitzgerald's, Esq., passing Listowel Bridge; the vale leading to it is very fine, the river is broad, the lands high, and one side a very extensive hanging wood, opening on those of Woodford in a pleasing style.

Woodford is an agreeable scene; close to the house is a fine winding river under a bank of thick wood, with the view of an old castle hanging over it.

In 1765, Mr. Fitzgerald was travelling from Constantinople to Warsaw, and a waggon with his baggage heavily laden overset; the country people harnessed two buffaloes by the horns, in order to draw it over, which they did with ease. In some very instructive conversation I had with this gentleman on the subject of his travels, this circumstance particularly struck me.

October 4. From Woodford to Tarbat, the seat of Edward Leslie, Esq., through a country rather dreary, till it came upon Tarbat, which is so much the contrary that it appeared to the highest advantage; the house is on the edge of a beautiful lawn, with a thick margin of full grown wood, hanging on a steep bank to the Shannon, so that the river is seen from the house over the tops of this wood, which being of a broken irregular outline has an effect very striking and uncommon; the river is two or three miles broad here, and the opposite coast forms a promontory which has from Tarbat exactly the appearance of a large island. To the east, the river swells into a triangular lake, with a reach opening at the distant corner of it to Limerick. The union of wood, water, and lawn forms upon the whole a very fine scene; the river is very magnificent. From the hill on the coast above the island, the lawn and wood appear also to great advantage. But the finest point of view is from the higher hill on the other side of the house, which looking down on all these scenes, they appear as a beautiful ornament to the Shannon, which spreads forth its proud course from two to nine miles wide, surrounded by highlands; a scenery truly magnificent.

The state of the poor is something better than it was twenty years ago, particularly their clothing, cattle, and cabins. They live upon potatoes and milk; all have cows, and when they dry them, buy others. They also have butter, and most of them keep pigs, killing them for their own use. They have also herrings. They are in general in the cottar system, of paying for labour by assigning some land to each cabin. The country is greatly more populous than twenty years ago, and is now increasing; and if ever so many cabins were built by a gradual increase, tenants would be found for them. A cabin and five acres of land will let for £4 a year. The industrious cottar, with two, three, or four acres, would be exceedingly glad to have his time to himself, and have such an annual addition of land as he was able to manage, paying a fair rent for it; none would decline it but the idle and worthless.

Tithes are all annually valued by the proctors, and charged very high. There are on the Shannon about one hundred boats employed in bringing turf to Limerick from the coast of Kerry and Clare, and in fishing; the former carry from twenty to twenty-five tons, the latter from five to ten, and are navigated each by two men and a boy.

October 5. Passed through a very unentertaining country (except for a few miles on the bank of the Shannon) to Altavilla, but Mr. Bateman being from home, I was disappointed in getting an account of the palatines settled in his neighbourhood. Kept the road to Adair, where Mrs. Quin, with a politeness equalled only by her understanding, procured me every intelligence I wished for.

Palatines were settled here by the late Lord Southwell about seventy years ago.

They preserve some of their German customs: sleep between two beds. They appoint a burgomaster, to whom they appeal in case of all disputes; and they yet preserve their language, but that is declining. They are very industrious, and in consequence are much happier and better fed, clothed, and lodged than the Irish peasants. We must not, however, conclude from hence that all is owing to this; their being independent farmers, and having leases, are circumstances which will create industry. Their crops are much better than those of their neighbours. There are three villages of them, about seventy families in all. For some time after they settled they fed upon sour-crout, but by degrees left it off, and took to potatoes; but now subsist upon them and butter and milk, but with a great deal of oat bread, and some of wheat, some meat and fowls, of which they raise many. They have all offices to their houses, that is, stables and cow-houses, and a lodge for their ploughs, etc. They keep their cows in the house in winter, feeding them upon hay and oat straw. They are remarkable for the goodness and cleanliness of their houses. The women are very industrious, reap the corn, plough the ground sometimes, and do whatever work may be going on; they also spin, and make their children do the same. Their wheat is much better than any in the country, insomuch that they get a better price than anybody else. Their industry goes so far, that jocular reports of its excess are spread. In a very pinching season, one of them yoked his wife against a horse, and went in that manner to work, and finished a journey at plough. The industry of the women is a perfect contrast to the Irish ladies in the cabins, who cannot be persuaded, on any consideration, even to make hay, it not being the custom of the country, yet they bind corn, and do other works more laborious. Mrs. Quin, who is ever attentive to introduce whatever can contribute to their welfare and happiness, offered many premiums to induce them to make hay, of hats, cloaks, stockings, etc. etc., but all would not do.

Few places have so much wood about them as Adair; Mr. Quin has above one thousand acres in his hands, in which a large proportion is under wood. The deer park of four hundred acres is almost full of old oak and very fine thorns, of a great size; and about the house, the plantations are very extensive, of elm and other wood, but that thrives better than any other sort. I have nowhere seen finer than vast numbers here. There is a fine river runs under the house, and within view are no less than three ruins of Franciscan friaries, two of them remarkably beautiful, and one has most of the parts perfect, except the roof.

In Mr. Quin's house there are some very good pictures, particularly an Annunciation by Domenichino, which is a beautiful piece. It was brought lately from Italy by Mr. Quin, junior. The colours are rich and mellow, and the hairs of the heads inimitably pleasing; the group of angels at the top, to the left of the piece, is very natural. It is a piece of great merit. The companion is a Magdalen; the expression of melancholy, or rather misery, remarkably strong.

There is a gloom in the whole in full unison with the subject. There are, besides these, some others inferior, yet of merit, and two very good portraits of Lord Dartry (Mrs. Quin's brother), and of Mr. Quin, junior, by Pompeio Battoni. A piece in an uncommon style, done on oak, of Esther and Ahasuerus; the colours tawdry, but the grouping attitudes and effect pleasing.

Castle Oliver is a place almost entirely of Mr. Oliver's creation; from a house, surrounded with cabins and rubbish, he has fixed it in a fine lawn, surrounded by good wood. The park he has very much improved on an excellent plan; by means of seven feet hurdles, he fences off part of it that wants to be cleaned or improved; these he cultivates, and leaves for grass, and then takes another spot, which is by much the best way of doing it. In the park is a glen, an English mile long, winding in a pleasing manner, with much wood hanging on the banks. Mr. Oliver has conducted a stream through this vale, and formed many little water-falls in an exceedingly good taste, chiefly overhung with wood, but in some places open with several little rills, trickling over stones down the slopes. A path winds through a large wood and along the brow of the glen; this path leads to a hermitage, a cave of rock, in a good taste, and to some benches, from which the views of the water and wood are in the sequestered style they ought to be. One of these little views, which catches several falls under the arch of the bridge, is one of the prettiest touches of the kind I have seen. The vale beneath the house, when viewed from the higher grounds, is pleasing; it is very well wooded, there being many inclosures, surrounded by pine trees, and a thick fine mass of wood rises from them up the mountain-side, makes a very good figure, and would be better, had not Mr. Oliver's father cut it into vistas for shooting. Upon the whole, the place is highly improved, and when the mountains are planted, in which Mr. Oliver is making a considerable progress, it will be magnificent.

In the house are several fine pictures, particularly five pieces by Seb. Ricci, Venus and Æneas; Apollo and Pan; Venus and Achilles; and Pyrrhus and Andromache, by Lazzerini; and the Rape of the Lapithi by the Centaurs. The last is by much the finest, and is a very capital piece; the expression is strong, the figures are in bold relief, and the colouring good. Venus and Achilles is a pleasing picture; the continence of Scipio is well grouped, but Scipio, as in every picture I ever saw of him, has no expression. Indeed, chastity is in the countenance so passive a virtue as not to be at all suited to the genius of painting; the idea is rather that of insipidity, and accordingly Scipio's expression is generally insipid enough. Two fine pieces, by Lucca Jordano, Hercules and Anteus; Samson Killing the Lion: both dark and horrid, but they are highly finished and striking. Six heads of old men, by Nagori, excellent; and four young women, in the character of the seasons.

October 9. Left Castle Oliver. Had I followed my inclination, my stay would have been much longer, for I found it equally the residence of entertainment and instruction. Passed through Kilfennan and Duntreleague, in my way to Tipperary. The road leads everywhere on the sides of the hills, so as to give a very distinct view of the lower grounds; the soil all the way is the same sort of sandy reddish loam I have already described, incomparable land for tillage: as I advanced it grew something lighter, and in many places free from gravel. Bullocks the stock all the way. Towards Tipperary I saw vast numbers of sheep, and many bullocks. All this line of country is part of the famous golden vale. To Thomas Town, where I was so unfortunate as not to find Mr. Matthew at home; the domain is one thousand five hundred English acres, so well planted that I could hardly believe myself in Ireland. There is a hill in the park from which the view of it, the country and the Galties, are striking.

October 12. To Lord de Montalt's, at Dundrum, a place which his lordship has ornamented in the modern style of improvement: the house was situated in the midst of all the regular exertions of the last age. Parterres, parapets of earth, straight walks, knots and clipped hedges, all which he has thrown down, with an infinite number of hedges and ditches, filled up ponds, etc., and opened one very noble lawn around him, scattered negligently over with trees, and cleared the course of a choked-up river, so that it flows at present in a winding course through the grounds.

October 13. Leaving Dundrum, passed through Cashel, where is a rock and ruin on it, called the Rock of Cashel, supposed to be of the remotest antiquity. Towards Clonmel, the whole way through the same rich vein of red sandy loam I have so often mentioned: I examined it in several fields, and found it to be of an extraordinary fertility, and as fine turnip land as ever I saw. It is much under sheep; but towards Clonmel there is a great deal of tillage.

The first view of that town, backed by a high ridge of mountains, with a beautiful space near it of inclosures, fringed with a scattering of trees, was very pleasing. It is the best situated place in the county of Tipperary, on the Suir, which brings up boats of ten tons burthen. It appears to be a busy populous place, yet I was told that the manufacture of woollens is not considerable. It is noted for being the birthplace of the inimitable Sterne.

To Sir William Osborne's, three miles the other side Clonmel. From a character so remarkable for intelligence and precision, I could not fail of meeting information of the most valuable kind. This gentleman has made a mountain improvement which demands particular attention, being upon a principle very different from common ones.

Twelve years ago he met with a hearty-looking fellow of forty, followed by a wife and six children in rags, who begged. Sir William questioned him upon the scandal of a man in full health and vigour, supporting himself in such a manner: the man said he could get no work: "Come along with me, I will show you a spot of land upon which I will build a cabin for you, and if you like it you shall fix there." The fellow followed Sir William, who was as good as his word: he built him a cabin, gave him five acres of a heathy mountain, lent him four pounds to stock with, and gave him, when he had prepared his ground, as much lime as he would come for. The fellow flourished; he went on gradually; repaid the four pounds, and presently became a happy little cottar: he has at present twelve acres under cultivation, and a stock in trade worth at least £80; his name is John Conory.

The success which attended this man in two or three years brought others who applied for land, and Sir William gave them as they applied. The mountain was under lease to a tenant, who valued it so little, that upon being reproached with not cultivating, or doing something with it, he assured Sir William that it was utterly impracticable to do anything with it, and offered it to him without any deduction of rent. Upon this mountain he fixed them; gave them terms as they came determinable with the lease of the farm, so that every one that came in succession had shorter and shorter tenures; yet are they so desirous of settling, that they come at present, though only two years remain for a term.

In this manner Sir William has fixed twenty-two families, who are all upon the improving hand, the meanest growing richer; and find themselves so well off, that no consideration will induce them to work for others, not even in harvest: their industry has no bounds; nor is the day long enough for the revolution of their incessant labour. Some of them bring turf to Clonmel, and Sir William has seen Conory returning loaded with soap ashes.

He found it difficult to persuade them to make a road to their village, but when they had once done it, he found none in getting cross roads to it, they found such benefit in the first. Sir William has continued to give whatever lime they come for: and they have desired one thousand barrels among them for the year 1766, which their landlord has accordingly contracted for with his lime-burner, at 11d. a barrel. Their houses have all been built at his expense, and done by contract at £6 each, after which they raise what little offices they want for themselves.

October 15. Left New Town, and keeping on the banks of the Suir, passed through Carrick to Curraghmore, the seat of the Earl of Tyrone. This line of country, in point of soil, inferior to what I have of late gone through: so that I consider the rich country to end at Clonmel.

Emigrations from this part of Ireland principally to Newfoundland: for a season they have £18 or £20 for their pay, and are maintained, but they do not bring home more than £7 to £11. Some of them stay and settle; three years ago there was an emigration of indented servants to North Carolina of three hundred, but they were stopped by contrary winds, etc. There had been something of this constantly, but not to that amount. The oppression which the poor people have most to complain of is the not having any tenures in their lands, by which means they are entirely subject to their employers.

Manufactures here are only woollens. Carrick is one of the greatest manufacturing towns in Ireland. Principally for ratteens, but of late they have got into broadcloths, all for home consumption; the manufacture increases, and is very flourishing. There are between three and four hundred people employed by it in Carrick and its neighbourhood.

Curraghmore is one of the finest places in Ireland, or indeed that I have anywhere seen. The house, which is large, is situated upon a rising ground, in a vale surrounded by very bold hills, which rise in a variety of forms and offer to the eye, in rising through the grounds, very noble and striking scenes. These hills are exceedingly varied, so that the detour of the place is very pleasing. In order to see it to advantage, I would advise a traveller to take the ride which Lord Tyrone carried me. Passed through the deer-park wood of old oaks, spread over the side of a bold hill, and of such an extent, that the scene is a truly forest one, without any other boundary in view than what the stems of trees offer from mere extent, retiring one behind another till they thicken so much to the eye, under the shade of their spreading tops, as to form a distant wall of wood. This is a sort of scene not common in Ireland; it is a great extent alone that will give it. From this hill enter an evergreen plantation, a scene which winds up the deer-park hill, and opens on to the brow of it, which commands a most noble view indeed. The lawns round the house appear at one's feet, at the bottom of a great declivity of wood, almost everywhere surrounded by

emigration

46

plantations. The hills on the opposite side of the vale against the house consist of a large lawn in the centre of the two woods, that to the right of an immense extent, which waves over a mountain-side in the finest manner imaginable, and lead the eye to the scenery on the left, which is a beautiful vale of rich inclosures, of several miles extent, with the Suir making one great reach through it, and a bold bend just before it enters a gap in the hills towards Waterford, and winds behind them; to the right you look over a large plain, backed by the great Cummeragh Mountains. For a distinct extent of view, the parts of which are all of a commanding magnitude, and a variety equal to the number, very few prospects are finer than this.

From hence the boundary plantation extends some miles to the west and north-west of the domain, forming a margin to the whole of different growths, having been planted, by degrees, from three to sixteen years. It is in general well grown, and the trees thriven exceedingly, particularly the oak, beech, larch, and firs. It is very well sketched, with much variety given to it.

Pass by the garden across the river which murmurs over a rocky bed, and follow the riding up a steep hill, covered with wood from some breaks, in which the house appears perfectly buried in a deep wood, and come out, after a considerable extent of ride, into the higher lawn, which commands a view of the scenery about the house; and from the brow of the hill the water, which is made to imitate a river, has a good effect, and throws a great air of cheerfulness over the scene, for from hence the declivity below it is hid. But the view, which is the most pleasing from hence, the finest at Curraghmore, and indeed one of the most striking that is anywhere to be seen, is that of the hanging wood to the right of the house, rising in so noble a sweep as perfectly to fill the eye, and leave the fancy scarce anything to wish: at the bottom is a small semicircular lawn, around which flows the river, under the immediate shade of very noble oaks. The whole wood rises boldly from the bottom, tree above tree, to a vast height, of large oak. The masses of shade are but tints of one colour; it is not chequered with a variety. There is a majestic simplicity, a unity in the whole, which is attended with an uncommon impression, and such as none but the most magnificent scenes can raise.

Descending from hence through the roads, the riding crosses the river, and passes through the meadow which has such an effect in the preceding scene, from which also the view is very fine, and leads home through a continued and an extensive range of fine oak, partly on a declivity, at the bottom of which the river murmurs its broken course.

Besides this noble riding, there is a very agreeable walk runs immediately on the banks of the river, which is perfect in its style; it is a sequestered line of wood, so high on the declivities in some places, and so thick on the very edge in others, overspreading the river, that the character of the scene is gloom and melancholy, heightened by the noise of the water falling from stone to stone. There is a considerable variety in the banks of it, and in the figures and growth of the wood, but none that hurts the impression, which is well preserved throughout.

October 17. Accompanied Lord Tyrone to Waterford; made some inquiries into the state of their trade, but found it difficult, from the method in which the custom-house books are kept, to get the details I wished; but in the year following, having the pleasure of a long visit at Ballycanvan, the seat of Cornelius Bolton, Esq., his son, the member for the city, procured me every information I could wish, and that in so liberal and polite a manner, that it would not be easy to express the obligations I am under to both. In general, I was informed that the trade of the place had increased considerably in ten years, both the exports and imports—the exports of the products of pasturage, full one-third in twelve years. That the staple trade of the place is the Newfoundland trade. This is very much increased; there is more of it here than anywhere. The number of people who go as passengers in the Newfoundland ships is amazing: from sixty to eighty ships, and from three thousand to five thousand annually. They come from most parts of Ireland, from Cork, Kerry, etc. Experienced men will get eighteen to twenty-five pounds for the season, from March to November. A man who never went will have five to seven pounds and his passage, and others rise to twenty pounds; the passage out they get, but pay home two pounds. An industrious man in a year will bring home twelve to sixteen pounds with him, and some more. A great point for them is to be able to carry out all their slops, for everything there is exceedingly dear, one or two hundred per cent. dearer than they can get them at home. They are not allowed to take out any woollen goods but for their own use. The ships go loaded with pork, beef, butter, and some salt; and bring home passengers, or get freights where they can; sometimes rum. The Waterford pork comes principally from the barony of Iverk, in Kilkenny, where they fatten great numbers of large hogs; for many weeks together they kill here three to four thousand a week, the price fifty shillings to four pounds each; goes chiefly to Newfoundland. One was killed in Mr. Penrose's cellar that weighed five hundredweight and a quarter, and measured from the nose to the end of the tail nine feet four inches.

There is a foundry at Waterford for pots, kettles, weights, and all common utensils; and a manufactory by Messrs. King and Tegent of anvils to anchors, twenty hundredweight, etc., which employs forty hands. Smiths earn from 6s. to 24s. a week. Nailers from 10s. to 12s. And another less considerable. There are two sugar-houses, and many salt-houses. The salt is boiled over lime-kilns.

There is a fishery upon the coast of Waterford, for a great variety of fish, herrings particularly, in the mouth of Waterford Harbour, and two years ago in such quantities there, that the tides left the ditches full of them. There are some premium boats both here and at Dungarvan, but the quantity of herrings barrelled is not considerable.

The butter trade of Waterford has increased greatly for seven years past; it comes from Waterford principally, but much from Carlow; for it comes from twenty miles beyond Carlow, for sixpence per hundred. From the 1st of January, 1774, to the 1st of January, 1775, there were exported fifty-nine thousand eight hundred and fifty-six casks of butter, each, on an average, one hundredweight, at the mean price of 50s. Revenue of Waterford, 1751, £17,000; 1776, £52,000. The slaughter trade has increased, but not so much as the butter. Price of butter now at Waterford, 58s.; twenty years' average, 42s. Beef now to 25s.; average, twenty years, 10s. to 18s. Pork, now 30s.; average, twenty years, 16s. to 22s. Eighty sail of ships now belonging to the port, twenty years ago not thirty. They pay to the captains of ship of two hundred tons £5 a month; the mate £3 10s. Ten men at 40s., five years ago only 27s. Building ships, £10 a ton. Wear and tear of such a ship, £20 a month. Ship provisions, 20s. a month.

The new church in this city is a very beautiful one; the body of it is in the same style exactly as that of Belfast, already described: the total length one hundred and seventy feet, the breadth fifty-eight. The length of the body of the church ninety-two, the height forty; breadth between the pillars, twenty-six. The aisle (which I do not remember at Belfast) is fifty-eight by forty-five. A room on one side the steeple, space for the bishop's court, twenty-four by eighteen; on the other side, a room of the same size for the vestry; and twenty-eight feet square left for a steeple when their funds will permit. The whole is light and beautiful. It was built by subscription, and there is a fine organ bespoke at London. But the finest object in this city is the quay, which is unrivalled by any I have seen. It is an English mile long; the buildings on it are only common houses, but the river is near a mile over, flows up to the town in one noble reach, and the opposite shore a bold hill, which rises immediately from the water to a height that renders the whole magnificent. This is scattered with some wood, and divided into pastures of a beautiful verdure by hedges. I crossed the water, in order to walk up the rocks on the top of this hill. In one place, over against Bilberry quarry, you look immediately down on the river, which flows in noble reaches from Granny Castle on the right past Cromwell's rock, the shores on both sides quite steep, especially the rock of Bilberry. You look over the whole town, which here appears in a triangular form. Besides the city the Cummeragh mountains, Slein-a-man, etc., come in view. Kilmacow river falls into the Suir, after flowing through a large extent of well-planted country. This is the finest view about the city.

From Waterford to Passage, and got my chaise and horses on board the Countess of Tyrone packet, in full expectation of sailing immediately, as the wind was fair, but I soon found the difference of these private vessels and the Post-Office packets at Holyhead and Dublin. When the wind was fair the tide was foul; and when the tide was with them the wind would not do. In English, there was not a complement of passengers, and so I had the agreeableness of waiting with my horses in the hold, by way of rest, after a journey of above one thousand five hundred miles.

October 18. After a beastly night passed on shipboard, and finding no signs of departure, walked to Ballycanvan, the seat of Cornelius Bolton, Esq.; rode with Mr. Bolton, jun., to Faithleghill, which commands one of the finest views I have seen in Ireland. There is a rock on the top of a hill which has a very bold view on every side down on a great extent of country, much of which is grass inclosures of a good verdure. This hill is the centre of a circle of about ten miles diameter, beyond which higher lands rise, which, after spreading to a great extent, have on every side a background of mountain: in a northerly direction Mount Leinster, between Wexford and Wicklow, twenty-six miles off, rises in several heads far above the clouds. A little to the right of this, Sliakeiltha (i.e. "the woody mountain"), at a less distance, is a fine object. To the left, Tory Hill, only five miles, in a regular form, varies the outline. To the east, there is the Long Mountain, eighteen miles distant, and several lesser Wexford hills. To the south-east, the Saltees. To the south, the ocean, and the Colines about the bay of Tramore. To the west, Monavollagh rises two thousand one hundred and sixty feet above the level of the sea, eighteen miles off, being part of the great range of the Cummeragh mountains: and to the north-west

Slein-a-man, at the distance of twenty-four miles; so that the outline is everywhere bold and distinct, though distant. These circumstances would alone form a great view, but the water part of it, which fills up the canvas, is in a much superior style. The great river Suir takes a winding course from the city of Waterford, through a rich country, hanging on the sides of hills to its banks, and, dividing into a double channel, forms the lesser island, both of which courses you command distinctly. United, it makes a bold reach under the hill on which you stand, and there receives the noble tribute of the united waters of the Barrow and Nore in two great channels, which form the larger island. Enlarged by such an accession of water, it winds round the hill in a bending course, of the freest and most graceful outline, everywhere from one to three miles across, with bold shores that give a sharp outline to its course to the ocean. Twenty sail of ships at Passage gave animation to the scene. Upon the whole, the boldness of the mountain outline, the variety of the grounds, the vast extent of river, with the declivity to it from the point of view, altogether form so unrivalled a scenery, every object so commanding, that the general want of wood is almost forgotten.

Two years after this account was written I again visited this enchanting hill, and walked to it, day after day, from Ballycanvan, and with increasing pleasure. Mr. Bolton, jun., has, since I was there before, inclosed forty acres on the top and steep slope to the water, and begun to plant them. This will be a prodigious addition; for the slope forming the bold shore for a considerable space, and having projections from which the wood will all be seen in the gentle hollows of the hill, the effect will be amazingly fine. Walks and a riding are tracing out, which will command fresh beauties at every step. The spots from which a variety of beautiful views are seen are numerous. All the way from Ballycanvan to Faithleg, the whole, to the amount of one thousand two hundred acres, is the property of Mr. Bolton.

Farms about Ballycanvan, Waterford, etc., are generally small, from twenty and thirty to five hundred acres, generally about two hundred and fifty. All above two hundred acres are in general dairies; some of the dairy ones rise very high. The soil is a reddish stony or slaty gravel, dry, except low lands, which are clay or turf. Rents vary much—about the town very high, from £5 5s. to £9, but at the distance of a few miles towards Passage, etc., they are from 20s. to 40s., and some higher, but the country in general does not rise so high, usually 10s. to 20s. for dairying land.

The poor people spin their own flax, but not more, and a few of them wool for themselves. Their food is potatoes and milk; but they have a considerable assistance from fish, particularly herrings; part of the year they have also barley, oaten, and rye bread. They are incomparably better off in every respect than twenty years ago. Their increase about Ballycanvan is very great, and tillage all over this neighbourhood is increased. The rent of a cabin 10s.; an acre with it 20s. The grass of a cow a few years ago 20s., now 25s. or 30s.

An exceeding good practice here in making their fences is, they plant the quick on the side of the bank in the common manner, and then, instead of the dead hedge we use in England on the top of the bank, they plant a row of old thorns, two or three feet high, which readily grow, and form at once a most excellent fence. Their way also of taking in sand-banks from the river deserves notice. They stake down a row of furzes at low water, laying stones on them to the height of one or two feet; these retain the mud, which every tide brings in, so as to fill up all within the furze as high as their tops. I remarked, on the strand, that a few boatloads of stones laid carelessly had had this effect, for within them I measured twelve inches deep of rich blue mud left behind them, the same as they use in manuring, full of shells, and effervesced strongly with vinegar.

Among the poor people the fishermen are in much the best circumstances. The fishery is considerable; Waterford and its harbour have fifty boats each, from eight to twelve tons, six men on an average to each, but to one of six tons five men go. A boat of eight tons costs £40; one of twelve, £60. To each boat there is a train of nets of six pair, which costs from £4 4s. to £6 6s.; tan them with bark. Their only net fishery is that of herrings, which is commonly carried on by shares. The division of the fish is, first, one-fourth for the boat; and then the men and nets divide the rest, the latter reckoned as three men. They reckon ten maze of herrings an indifferent night's work; when there is a good take, forty maze have been taken, twenty a good night; the price per maze from 1s. to 7s., average 5s. Their take in 1775, the greatest they have known, when they had more than they could dispose of, and the whole town and country stunk of them, they retailed them thirty-two for a penny; 1773 and 1774 good years. They barrelled many, but in general there is an import of Swedish. Besides the common articles I have registered, the following are: pigeons, 1s. a couple; a hare, 1s.; partridges, 9d.; turbots, fine ones, 4s. to 10s.; soles a pair, large, 1s. 6d to 1s.; lobsters, 3d. each; oysters, 6s. per hundred; rabbits, 1s. to 1s. 4d. a couple; cod, 1s. each, large; salmon, 1¼d. to 2d.

A very extraordinary circumstance I was told—that within five or six years there has been much hay carried from Waterford to Norway, in the Norway ships that bring deals. As hay is dear here, it proves a most backward state of husbandry in that northerly region, since the neighbourhood of sea-ports to which this hay can alone go is generally the best improved in all countries.

October 19, the wind being fair, took my leave of Mr. Bolton, and went back to the ship. Met with a fresh scene of provoking delays, so that it was the next morning, October 20, at eight o'clock, before we sailed, and then it was not wind, but a cargo of passengers that spread our sails. Twelve or fourteen hours are not an uncommon passage, but such was our luck that, after being in sight of the lights on the Smalls, we were by contrary winds blown opposite to Arklow sands. A violent gale arose, which presently blew a storm that lasted thirty-six hours, in which, under a reefed mainsail, the ship drifted up and down wearing in order to keep clear of the coasts.

No wonder this appeared to me, a fresh-water sailor, as a storm, when the oldest men on board reckoned it a violent one. The wind blew in furious gusts; the waves ran very high; the cabin windows burst open, and the sea pouring in set everything afloat, and among the rest a poor lady, who had spread her bed on the floor. We had, however, the satisfaction to find, by trying the pumps every watch, that the ship made little water. I had more time to attend these circumstances than the rest of the passengers, being the only one in seven who escaped without being sick. It pleased God to preserve us, but we did not cast anchor in Milford Haven till Tuesday morning, the 22nd, at one o'clock.

It is much to be wished that there were some means of being secure of packets sailing regularly, instead of waiting till there is such a number of passengers as satisfies the owner and captain. With the Post-Office packets there is this satisfaction, and a great one it is. The contrary conduct is so perfectly detestable that I should suppose the scheme of Waterford ones can never succeed.

Two years after, having been assured this conveyance was put on a new footing, I ventured to try it again, but was mortified to find that the Tyrone, the only one that could take a chaise or horses (the Countess being laid up), was repairing, but would sail in five days. I waited, and received assurance after assurance that she would be ready on such a day, and then on another. In a word, I waited twenty-four days before I sailed. Moderately speaking, I could by Dublin have reached Turin or Milan as soon as I did Milford in this conveyance. All this time the papers had constant advertisements of the Tyrone sailing regularly, instead of letting the public know that she was under a repair. Her owner seems to be a fair and worthy man; he will therefore probably give up the scheme entirely, unless assisted by the corporation with at least four ships more, to sail regularly with or without passengers. At present it is a general disappointment. I was fortunate in Mr. Bolton's acquaintance, passing my time very agreeably at his hospitable mansion; but those who, in such a case, should find a Waterford inn their resource, would curse the Tyrone, and set off for Dublin. The expenses of this passage are higher than those from Dublin to Holyhead: I paid—

* * * * *

1777. Upon a second journey to Ireland this year, I took the opportunity of going from Dublin to Mitchelstown, by a route through the central part of the kingdom, which I had not before sufficiently viewed.

Left Dublin the 24th of September, and taking the road to Naas, I was again struck with the great population of the country, the cabins being so much poorer in the vicinity of the capital than in the more distant parts of the kingdom.

To Kildare, crossing the Curragh, so famous for its turf. It is a sheep-walk of above four thousand English acres, forming a more beautiful lawn than the hand of art ever made. Nothing can exceed the extreme softness of the turf, which is of a verdure that charms the eye, and highly set off by the gentle inequality of surface. The soil is a fine dry loam on a stony bottom; it is fed by many large flocks, turned on it by the occupiers of the adjacent farms, who alone have the right, and pay very great rents on that account. It is the only considerable common in the kingdom. The sheep yield very little wool, not more than 3lb. per fleece, but of a very fine quality.

From Furness to Shaen Castle, in the Queen's County, Dean Coote's; but as the husbandry, etc., of this neighbourhood is already registered, I have only to observe that Mr. Coote was so kind as to show me the improved grounds of Dawson's Court, the seat of Lord Carlow, which I had not seen before. The principal beauties of the place are the well-grown and extensive plantations, which form a shade not often met with in Ireland. There is in the backgrounds a lake well accompanied with wood, broken by several islands that are covered with underwood, and an ornamented walk passing on the banks which leads from the house. This lake is in the season perfectly alive with wild-fowl. Near it is a very beautiful spot, which commands a view of both woods and water; a situation either for a house or a temple. Mr. Dawson is adding to the plantations, an employment of all others the most meritorious in Ireland. Another work, scarcely less so, was the erecting a large handsome inn, wherein the same gentleman intends establishing a person who shall be able to supply travellers post with either chaises or horses.

From Shaen Castle to Gloster, in the King's County, the seat of John Lloyd, Esq., member for that county, to whose attention I owe the following particulars, in which he took every means to have me well and accurately informed. But first let me observe that I was much pleased to remark, all the way from Naas quite to Rosscrea, that the country was amongst the finest I had seen in Ireland, and consequently that I was fortunate in having an opportunity of seeing it after the involuntary omission of last year. The cabins, though many of them are very bad, yet are better than in some other counties, and chimneys generally a part of them. The people, too, have no very miserable appearance; the breed of cattle and sheep good, and the hogs much the best I have anywhere seen in Ireland. Turf is everywhere at hand, and in plenty; yet are the bogs not so general as to affect the beauty of the country, which is very great in many tracts, with a scattering of wood, which makes it pleasing. Shaen Castle stands in the midst of a very fine tract. From Mountrath to Gloster, Mr. Lloyd's, I could have imagined myself in a very pleasing part of England. The country breaks into a variety of inequalities of hill and dale; it is all well inclosed with fine hedges; there is a plenty of wood, not so monopolised as in many parts of the kingdom by here and there a solitary seat, but spread over the whole face of the prospect: look which way you will, it is cultivated and cheerful.

The Shannon adds not a little to the convenience and agreeableness of a residence so near it. Besides affording these sorts of wild-fowl, the quantity and size of its fish are amazing: pikes swarm in it, and rise in weight to fifty pounds. In the little flat spaces on its banks are small but deep lochs, which are covered in winter and in floods. When the river withdraws, it leaves plenty of fish in them, which are caught to put into stews. Mr. Holmes has a small one before his door at Johnstown, with a little stream which feeds it. A trowling-rod here gets you a bite in a moment, of a pike from twenty to forty pounds. I ate of one of twenty-seven pounds so taken. I had also the pleasure of seeing a fisherman bring three trout, weighing fourteen pounds, and sell them for sixpence-halfpenny a piece. A couple of boats lying at anchor, with lines extended from one to the other, and hooks in plenty from them, have been known to catch an incredible quantity of trout. Colonel Prittie, in one morning, caught four stone odd pounds, thirty-two trout. In general they rise from three to nine pounds. Perch swarm; they appeared in the Shannon for the first time about ten years ago, in such plenty that the poor lived on them. Bream of six pounds; eels very plentiful. There are many gillaroos in the river; one of twelve pounds weight was sent to Mr. Jenkinson. Upon the whole, these circumstances, with the pleasure of shooting and boating on the river, added to the glorious view it yields, and which is enough at any time to cheer the mind, render this neighbourhood one of the most enviable situations to live in that I have seen in Ireland. The face of the country gives every circumstance of beauty. From Killodeernan Hill, behind the new house building by Mr. Holmes, the whole is seen to great advantage. The spreading part of the Shannon, called Loch Derg, is commanded distinctly for many miles. It is in two grand divisions of great variety: that to the north is a reach of five miles leading to Portumna. The whole hither shore a scenery of hills, checkered by enclosures and little woods, and retiring from the eye into a rich distant prospect. The woods of Doras, belonging to Lord Clanricarde, form a part of the opposite shore, and the river itself presents an island of one hundred and twenty acres. Inclining to the left, a vale of rough ground, with an old castle in it, is backed by a bold hill, which intercepts the river there, and then the great reach of fifteen miles, the bay of Sheriff, spreads to the eye, with a magnificence not a little added to by the boundary, a sharp outline of the county of Clare mountains, between which and the Duharrow hills the Shannon finds its way. These hills lead the eye still more to the left, till the Keeper meets it, presenting a very beautiful outline that sinks into other ranges of hill, uniting with the Devil's Bit. The home scenery of the grounds, woods, hills, and lake of Johnstown, is beautiful.

Dancing is very general among the poor people, almost universal in every cabin. Dancing-masters of their own rank travel through the country from cabin to cabin, with a piper or blind fiddler, and the pay is sixpence a quarter. It is an absolute system of education. Weddings are always celebrated with much dancing, and a Sunday rarely passes without a dance. There are very few among them who will not, after a hard day's work, gladly walk seven miles to have a dance. John is not so lively, but then a hard day's work with him is certainly a different affair from what it is with Paddy. Other branches of education are likewise much attended to, every child of the poorest family learning to read, write, and cast accounts.

There is a very ancient custom here, for a number of country neighbours among the poor people to fix upon some young woman that ought, as they think, to be married. They also agree upon a young fellow as a proper husband for her. This determined, they send to the fair one's cabin to inform her that on the Sunday following "she is to be horsed," that is, carried on men's backs. She must then provide whisky and cider for a treat, as all will pay her a visit after mass for a hurling match. As soon as she is horsed, the hurling begins, in which the young fellow appointed for her husband has the eyes of all the company fixed on him. If he comes off conqueror, he is certainly married to the girl; but if another is victorious, he as certainly loses her, for she is the prize of the victor. These trials are not always finished in one Sunday; they take sometimes two or three, and the common expression when they are over is, that "such a girl was goaled." Sometimes one barony hurls against another, but a marriageable girl is always the prize. Hurling is a sort of cricket, but instead of throwing the ball in order to knock down a wicket, the aim is to pass it through a bent stick, the end stuck in the ground. In these matches they perform such feats of activity as ought to evidence the food they live on to be far from deficient in nourishment.

In the hills above Derry are some very fine slate quarries, that employ sixty men. The quarrymen are paid 3s. a thousand for the slates, and the labourers 5d. a day. They are very fine, and sent by the Shannon to distant parts of the kingdom; the price at the quarry 6s. a thousand, and at the shore 6s. 8d. Four hundred thousand slates are raised to pay the rent only, from which some estimate may be made of the quantity.

Mr. Head has a practice in his fences which deserves universal imitation; it is planting trees for gate-posts. Stone piers are expensive, and always tumbling down; trees are beautiful, and never want repairing. Within fifteen years this gentleman has improved Derry so much, that those who had only seen it before would find it almost a new creation. He has built a handsome stone house, on the slope of a hill rising from the Shannon, and backed by some fine woods, which unite with many old hedges well planted to form a woodland scene beautiful in the contrast to the bright expanse of the noble river below. The declivity on which these woods are finishes in a mountain, which rises above the whole. The Shannon gives a bend around the adjoining lands, so as to be seen from the house both to the west and north, the lawn falling gradually to a margin of wood on the shore, which varies the outline. The river is two miles broad, and on the opposite shore cultivated inclosures rise in some places almost to the mountain top, which is very bold.

It is a very singular demesne; a stripe of very beautiful ground, reaching two miles along the banks of the river, which forms his fence on one side, with a wall on the other. There is so much wood as to render it very pleasing; adding to every day by planting all the fences made or repaired. From several little hills, which rise in different parts of it, extensive views of the river are commanded quite to Portumna; but these are much eclipsed by that from the top of the hill above the slate quarry. From thence you see the river for at least forty miles, from Portumna to twenty miles beyond Limerick. It has the appearance of a fine basin, two miles over, into which three great rivers lead, being the north and south course and the Bay of Sheriff. The reaches of it one beyond another to Portumna are fine. At the foot of the mountain Mr. Head's demesne extends in a shore of rich woodland.

October 7. Took my leave of Mr. Head, after passing four days very agreeably. Through Killaloe, over the Shannon, a very long bridge of many arches; went out of the road to see a fall of that river at Castle Connel, where there is such an accompaniment of wood as to form a very pleasing scenery. The river takes a very rapid rocky course around a projecting rock, on which a gentleman has built a summer-house, and formed a terrace: it is a striking spot. To Limerick. Laid at Bennis's, the first inn we had slept in from Dublin. God preserve us this journey from another!

It is not uncommon, especially in mountainous countries, to find objects that much deserve the attention of travellers entirely neglected by them. There are a few instances of this upon Lord Kingsborough's estate, in the neighbourhood of Mitchelstown. The first I shall mention is a cave at Skeheenrinky, on the road between Cahir and that place. The opening to it is a cleft of rock in a limestone hill, so narrow as to be difficult to get into it. I descended by a ladder of about twenty steps, and then found myself in a vault of a hundred feet long, and fifty or sixty high. A small hole on the left leads from this a winding course of I believe not less than half an Irish mile, exhibiting a variety that struck me much. In some places the cavity in the rock is so large that when well lighted up by candles (not flambeaux; Lord Kingsborough once showed it me with them, and we found their smoke troublesome) it takes the appearance of a vaulted cathedral, supported by massy columns. The walls, ceiling, floor, and pillars, are by turns composed of every fantastic form; and often of very beautiful incrustations of spar, some of which glitters so much that it seems powdered with diamonds; and in others the ceiling is formed of that sort which has so near a resemblance to a cauliflower. The spar formed into columns by the dropping of water has taken some very regular forms; but others are different, folded in plaits of light drapery, which hang from their support in a very pleasing manner. The angles of the walls seem fringed with icicles. One very long branch of the cave, which turns to the north, is in some places so narrow and low, that one crawls into it, when it suddenly breaks into large vaulted spaces, in a thousand forms. The spar in all this cave is very brilliant, and almost equal to Bristol stone. For several hundred yards in the larger branch there is a deep water at the bottom of the declivity to the right, which the common people call the river. A part of the way is over a sort of potter's clay, which moulds into any form, and is of a brown colour; a very different soil from any in the neighbouring country. I have seen the famous cave in the Peak, but think it very much inferior to this; and Lord Kingsborough, who has viewed the Grot d'Aucel in Burgundy, says that it is not to be compared with it.

But the commanding region of the Galtees deserves more attention. Those who are fond of scenes in which Nature reigns in all her wild magnificence should visit this stupendous chain. It consists of many vast mountains, thrown together in an assemblage of the most interesting features, from the boldness and height of the declivities, freedom of outline, and variety of parts, filling a space of about six miles by three or four. Galtymore is the highest point, and rises like the lord and father of the surrounding progeny. From the top you look down upon a great extent of mountain, which shelves away from him to the south, east, and west; but to the north the ridge is almost a perpendicular declivity. On that side the famous golden vale of Limerick and Tipperary spreads a rich level to the eye, bounded by the mountains of Clare, King's and Queen's Counties, with the course of the Shannon, for many miles below Limerick. To the south you look over alternate ridges of mountains, which rise one beyond another, till in a clear day the eye meets the ocean near Dungarvan. The mountains of Waterford and Knockmealdown fill up the space to the south-east. The western is the most extensive view; for nothing stops the eye till Mangerton and Macgillicuddy Reeks point out the spot where Killarney's lake calls for a farther excursion. The prospect extends into eight counties—Cork, Kerry, Waterford, Limerick, Clare, Queen's, Tipperary, King's.

A little to the west of this proud summit, below it in a very extraordinary hollow, is a circular lake of two acres, reported to be unfathomable. The descriptions which I have read of the craters of exhausted volcanoes leave very little doubt of this being one; and the conical regularity of the summit of Galtymore speaks the same language. East of this respectable hill, to use Sir William Hamilton's language, is a declivity of about one-quarter of a mile, and there Galtybeg rises in a yet more regular cone; and between the two hills is another lake, which from its position seems to have been once the crater which threw up Galtybeg, as the first mentioned was the origin of

Galtymore. Beyond the former hill is a third lake, and east of that another hill; I was told of a fourth, with another corresponding mountain. It is only the mere summits of these mountains which rise above the lakes. Speaking of them below, they may be said to be on the tops of the hills. They are all of them at the bottom of an almost regularly circular hollow. On the side next the mountain-top are walls of perpendicular rocks, in regular strata, and some of them piled on each other, with an appearance of art rather than nature. In these rocks the eagles, which are seen in numbers on the Galtees, have their nests. Supposing the mountains to be of volcanic origin, and these lakes the craters, of which I have not a doubt, they are objects of the greatest curiosity, for there is an unusual regularity in every considerable summit having its corresponding crater. But without this circumstance, the scenery is interesting in a very great degree. The mountain summits, which are often wrapped in the clouds, at other times exhibit the freest outline; the immense scooped hollows which sink at your feet, declivities of so vast a depth as to give one terror to look down; with the unusual forms of the lower region of hills, particularly Bull Hill, and Round Hill, each a mile over, yet rising out of circular vales, with the regularity of semi-globes, unite upon the whole to exhibit a scenery to the eye in which the parts are of a magnitude so commanding, a character so interesting, and a variety so striking, that they well deserve to be examined by every curious traveller.

Nor are these immense outlines the whole of what is to be seen in this great range of mountains. Every glen has its beauties: there is a considerable mountain river, or rather torrent, in every one of them; but the greatest are the Funcheon, between Sefang and Galtymore; the Limestone river, between Galtymore and Round Hill, and the Grouse river, between Coolegarranroe and Mr. O'Callaghan's mountain; these present to the eye, for a tract of about three miles, every variety that rock, water, and mountain can give, thrown into all the fantastic forms which art may attempt in ornamented grounds, but always fails in. Nothing can exceed the beauty of the water, when not discoloured by rain; its lucid transparency shows, at considerable depths, every pebble no bigger than a pin, every rocky basin alive with trout and eels, that play and dash among the rocks as if endowed with that native vigour which animates, in a superior degree, every inhabitant of the mountains, from the bounding red deer and the soaring eagle down even to the fishes of the brook. Every five minutes you have a water-fall in these glens, which in any other region would stop every traveller to admire it. Sometimes the vale takes a gentle declivity, and presents to the eye at one stroke twenty or thirty falls, which render the scenery all alive with motion; the rocks are tossed about in the wildest confusion, and the torrent bursts by turns from above, beneath, and under them; while the background is always filled up with the mountains which stretch around.

In the western glen is the finest cascade in all the Galtees. There are two falls, with a basin in the rock between, but from some points of view they appear one: the rock over which the water tumbles is about sixty feet high. A good line in which to view these objects is either to take the Killarney and Mallow road to Mitchelstown and from thence by Lord Kingsborough's new one to Skeheenrinky, there to take one of the glens to Galtybeg and Galtymore, and return to Mitchelstown by the Wolf's Track, Temple Hill, and the Waterfall; or, if the Cork road is travelling, to make Dobbin's inn, at Ballyporeen, the head-quarters, and view them from thence.

* * * * *

Having heard much of the beauties of a part of the Queen's County I had not before seen, I took that line of country in my way on a journey to Dublin.

From Mitchelstown to Cashel, the road leads as far as Galbally in the route already travelled from Cullen. Towards Cashel the country is various. The only objects deserving attention are the plantations of Thomastown, the seat of Francis Mathew, Esq.; they consist chiefly of hedgerow trees in double and treble rows, are well grown, and of such extent as to form an uncommon woodland scene in Ireland. Found the widow Holland's inn, at Cashel, clean and very civil. Take the road to Urlingford. The rich sheep pastures, part of the famous golden vale, reach between three and four miles from Cashel to the great bog by Botany Hill, noted for producing a greater variety of plants than common. That bog is separated by only small tracts of land from the string of bogs which extend through the Queen's County, from the great bog of Allen; it is here of considerable extent, and exceedingly improvable. Then enter a low marshy bad country, which grows worse after passing the sixty-sixth milestone, and successive bogs in it. Breakfast at Johnstown, a regular village on a slight eminence, built by Mr. Hayley. It is near the spa of Ballyspellin.

Rows of trees are planted, but their heads all cut off, I suppose from their not thriving, being planted too old. Immediately on leaving these planted avenues, enter a row of eight or ten new cabins, at a distance from each other, which appear to be a new undertaking, the land about them all pared and burnt, and the ashes in heaps.

Enter a fine planted country, with much corn and good thriving quick hedges for many miles. The road leads through a large wood, which joins Lord Ashbrook's plantations, whose house is situated in the midst of more wood than almost any one I have seen in Ireland. Pass Durrow; the country for two or three miles continues all inclosed with fine quick hedges, is beautiful, and has some resemblance to the best parts of Essex. Sir Robert Staple's improvements join this fine tract. They are completed in a most perfect manner, the hedges well grown, cut, and in such excellent order that I can scarcely believe myself to be in Ireland. His gates are all of iron. These sylvan scenes continue through other seats, beautifully situated amidst gentle declivities of the finest verdure, full-grown woods, excellent hedges, and a pretty river winding by the house. The whole environs of several would be admired in the best parts of England.

Cross a great bog, within sight of Lord de Vesci's plantations. The road leads over it, being drained for that purpose by deep cuts on either side. I should apprehend this bog to be among the most improvable in the country. Slept at Ballyroan, at an inn kept by three animals who call themselves women; met with more impertinence than at any other in Ireland. It is an execrable hole. In three or four miles pass Sir John Parnel's, prettily situated in a neatly dressed lawn, with much wood about it, and a lake quite alive with wild fowl.

Pass Monstereven, and cross directly a large bog, drained and partly improved; but all of it bearing grass, and seems in a state that might easily be reduced to rich meadow, with only a dressing of lime. Here I got again into the road I had travelled before.

I must in general remark, that from near Urlingford to Dawson Court, near Monstereven, which is completely across the Queen's County, is a line of above thirty English miles, and is for that extent by much the most improved of any I have seen in Ireland. It is generally well planted, has many woods, and not consisting of patches of plantation just by gentlemen's houses, but spreading over the whole face of the country, so as to give it the richness of an English woodland scene. What a country would Ireland be had the inhabitants of the rest of it improved the whole like this!

If only all Ireland looked this like this

PART II.: SECTION I.—Soil, Face of the Country, and Climate.

To judge of Ireland by the conversation one sometimes hears in England, it would be supposed that one-half of it was covered with bogs, and the other with mountains filled with Irish ready to fly at the sight of a civilised being. There are people who will smile when they hear that, in proportion to the size of the two countries, Ireland is more cultivated than England, having much less waste land of all sorts. Of uncultivated mountains there are no such tracts as are found in our four northern counties, and the North Riding of Yorkshire, with the eastern line of Lancaster, nearly down to the Peak of Derby, which form an extent of above a hundred miles of waste. The most considerable of this sort in Ireland are in Kerry, Galway, and Mayo, and some in Sligo and Donegal. But all these together will not make the quantity we have in the four northern counties; the valleys in the Irish mountains are also more inhabited, I think, than those of England, except where there are mines, and consequently some sort of cultivation creeping up the sides. Natural fertility, acre for acre over the two kingdoms, is certainly in favour of Ireland; of this I believe there can scarcely be a doubt entertained, when it is considered that some of the more beautiful, and even best cultivated counties in England, owe almost everything to the capital, art, and industry of the inhabitants.

The circumstance which strikes me as the greatest singularity of Ireland is the rockiness of the soil, which should seem at first sight against that degree of fertility; but the contrary is the fact. Stone is so general, that I have great reason to believe the whole island is one vast rock of different strata and kinds rising out of the sea. I have rarely heard of any great depths being sunk without meeting with it. In general it appears on the surface in every part of the kingdom; the flattest and most fertile parts, as Limerick, Tipperary, and Meath, have it at no great depth, almost as much as the more barren ones. May we not recognise in this the hand of bounteous Providence, which has given perhaps the most stony soil in Europe to the moistest climate in it? If as much rain fell upon the clays of England (a soil very rarely met with in Ireland, and never without much stone) as falls upon the rocks of her sister island, those lands could not be cultivated. But the rocks are here clothed with verdure; those of limestone, with only a thin covering of mould, have the softest and most beautiful turf imaginable.

Of the great advantages resulting from the general plenty of limestone and limestone gravel, and the nature of the bogs, I shall have occasion to speak more particularly hereafter.

The rockiness of the soil in Ireland is so universal that it predominates in every sort. One cannot use with propriety the terms clay, loam, sand, etc.; it must be a stony clay, a stony loam, a gravelly sand. Clay, especially the yellow, is much talked of in Ireland, but it is for want of proper discrimination. I have once or twice seen almost a pure clay upon the surface, but it is extremely rare. The true yellow clay is usually found in a thin stratum under the surface mould, and over a rock; harsh, tenacious, stony, strong loams, difficult to work, are not uncommon: but they are quite different from English clays.

Friable, sandy loams, dry but fertile, are very common, and they form the best soils in the kingdom for tillage and sheep. Tipperary and Roscommon abound particularly in them. The most fertile of all are the bullock pastures of Limerick, and the banks of the Shannon in Clare, called the Corcasses. These are a mellow, putrid, friable loam.

Sand which is so common in England, and yet more common through Spain, France, Germany, and Poland, quite from Gibraltar to Petersburg, is nowhere met with in Ireland, except for narrow slips of hillocks, upon the sea coast. Nor did I ever meet with or hear of a chalky soil.

The bogs, of which foreigners have heard so much, are very extensive in Ireland; that of Allen extends eighty miles, and is computed to contain three hundred thousand acres. There are others also, very extensive, and smaller ones scattered over the whole kingdom; but these are not in general more than are wanted for fuel. When I come to speak of the improvement of waste lands, I shall describe them particularly.

Besides the great fertility of the soil, there are other circumstances which come within my sphere to mention. Few countries can be better watered by large and beautiful rivers; and it is remarkable that by much the finest parts of the kingdom are on the banks of these rivers. Witness the Suir, Blackwater, the Liffey, the Boyne, the Nore, the Barrow, and part of the Shannon, they wash a scenery that can hardly be exceeded. From the rockiness of the country, however, there are few of them that have not obstructions, which are great impediments to inland navigation.

The mountains of Ireland give to travelling that interesting variety which a flat country can never abound with. And, at the same time, they are not in such number as to confer the usual character of poverty which attends them. I was either upon or very near the most considerable in the kingdom. Mangerton, and the Reeks, in Kerry; the Galties in Cork; those of Mourne in Down; Crow Patrick, and Nephin in Mayo, these are the principal in Ireland, and they are of a character, in height and sublimity, which should render them the objects of every traveller's attention.

Relative to the climate of Ireland, a short residence cannot enable a man to speak much from his own experience; the observations I have made myself confirm the idea of its being vastly wetter than England; from the 20th of June to the 20th of October I kept a register, and there were, in one hundred and twenty-two days, seventy-five of rain, and very many of them incessant and heavy. I have examined similar registers I kept in England, and can find no year that even approaches to such a moisture as this. But there is a register of an accurate diary published which compares London and Cork. The result is, that the quantity at the latter place was double to that at London. See Smith's "History of Cork."

From the information I received, I have reason to believe that the rainy season sets in usually about the first of July and continues very wet till September or October, when there is usually a dry fine season of a month or six weeks. I resided in the county of Cork, etc., from October till March, and found the winter much more soft and mild than ever I experienced one in England. I was also a whole summer there (1778), and it is fair to mention that it was as fine a one as ever I knew in England, though by no means so hot. I think hardly so wet as very many I have known in England. The tops of the Galty mountains exhibited the only snow we saw; and as to frosts, they were so slight and rare that I believe myrtles, and yet tenderer plants, would have survived without any covering. But when I say that the winter was not remarkable for being wet, I do not mean that we had a dry atmosphere. The inches of rain which fell in the winter I speak of would not mark the moisture of the climate. As many inches will fall in a single tropical shower as in a whole year in England. See Mitchel's "Present State of Great Britain and North America." But if the clouds presently disperse, and a bright sun shines, the air may soon be dry. The worst circumstance of the climate of Ireland is the constant moisture without rain. Wet a piece of leather, and lay it in a room where there is neither sun nor fire, and it will not in summer even be dry in a month. I have known gentlemen in Ireland deny their climate being moister than England, but if they have eyes let them open them, and see the verdure that clothes their rocks, and compare it with ours in England—where rocky soils are of a russet brown however sweet the food for sheep. Does not their island lie more exposed to the great Atlantic; and does not the west wind blow three-fourths of a year? If there was another island yet more westward, would not the climate of Ireland be improved? Such persons speak equally against fact, reason, and philosophy. That the moisture of a climate does not depend on the quantity of rain that falls, but on the powers of aerial evaporation, Dr. Dobson has clearly proved. "Phil. Trans." vol. lxvii., part i., p. 244.

Class [handwritten]

Oppression.

Before I conclude this article of the common labouring poor in Ireland, I must observe, that their happiness depends not merely upon the payment of their labour, their clothes, or their food; the subordination of the lower classes, degenerating into oppression, is not to be overlooked. The poor in all countries, and under all governments, are both paid and fed, yet there is an infinite difference between them in different ones. This inquiry will by no means turn out so favourable as the preceding articles. It must be very apparent to every traveller through that country, that the labouring poor are treated with harshness, and are in all respects so little considered that their want of importance seems a perfect contrast to their situation in England, of which country, comparatively speaking, they reign the sovereigns. The age has improved so much in humanity, that even the poor Irish have experienced its influence, and are every day treated better and better; but still the remnant of the old manners, the abominable distinction of religion, united with the oppressive conduct of the little country gentlemen, or rather vermin of the kingdom, who never were out of it, altogether bear still very heavy on the poor people, and subject them to situations more mortifying than we ever behold in England. The landlord of an Irish estate, inhabited by Roman Catholics, is a sort of despot who yields obedience, in whatever concerns the poor, to no law but that of his will. To discover what the liberty of the people is, we must live among them, and not look for it in the statutes of the realm: the language of written law may be that of liberty, but the situation of the poor may speak no language but that of slavery. There is too much of this contradiction in Ireland; a long series of oppressions, aided by many very ill-judged laws, have brought landlords into a habit of exerting a very lofty superiority, and their vassals into that of an almost unlimited submission: speaking a language that is despised, professing a religion that is abhorred and being disarmed, the poor find themselves in many cases slaves even in the bosom of written liberty. Landlords that have resided much abroad are usually humane in their ideas, but the habit of tyranny naturally contracts the mind, so that even in this polished age there are instances of a severe carriage towards the poor, which is quite unknown in England.

liberty! [handwritten margin note]

history. [handwritten margin note]

A landlord in Ireland can scarcely invent an order which a servant, labourer, or cottar dares to refuse to execute. Nothing satisfies him but an unlimited submission. Disrespect, or anything tending towards sauciness, he may punish with his cane or his horsewhip with the most perfect security; a poor man would have his bones broke if he offered to lift his hands in his own defence. Knocking-down is spoken of in the country in a manner that makes an Englishman stare. Landlords of consequence have assured me that many of their cottars would think themselves honoured by having their wives and daughters sent for to the bed of their master; a mark of slavery that proves the oppression under which such people must live. Nay, I have heard anecdotes of the lives of people being made free with without any apprehension of the justice of a jury. But let it not be imagined that this is common; formerly it happened every day, but law gains ground. It must strike the most careless traveller to see whole strings of cars whipped into a ditch by a gentleman's footman to make way for his carriage; if they are overturned or broken in pieces, no matter, it is taken in patience; were they to complain they would perhaps be horsewhipped. The execution of the laws lies very much in the hands of justices of the peace, many of whom are drawn from the most illiberal class in the kingdom. If a poor man lodges a complaint against a gentleman, or any animal that chooses to call itself a gentleman, and the justice issues out a summons for his appearance, it is a fixed affront, and he will infallibly be called out. Where manners are in conspiracy against law, to whom are the oppressed people to have recourse? It is a fact, that a poor man having a contest with a gentleman, must—but I am talking nonsense, they know their situation too well to think of it; they can have no defence, but by means of protection from one gentleman against another, who probably protects his vassal as he would the sheep he intends to eat.

The colours of this picture are not charged. To assert that all these cases are common would be an exaggeration, but to say that an unfeeling landlord will do all this with impunity, is to keep strictly to truth: and what is liberty but a farce and a jest, if its blessings are received as the favour of kindness and humanity, instead of being the inheritance of right?

Consequences have flowed from these oppressions which ought long ago to have put a stop to them. In England we have heard much of White-boys, Steel-boys, Oak-boys, Peep-of-day-boys, etc. But these various insurgents are not to be confounded, for they are very different. The proper distinction in the discontents of the people is into Protestant and Catholic. All but the White-boys were among the manufacturing Protestants in the north: the White-boys Catholic labourers in the south. From the best intelligence I could gain, the riots of the manufacturers had no other foundation but such variations in the manufacture as all fabrics experience, and which they had themselves known and submitted to before. The case, however, was different with the White-boys, who being labouring Catholics met with all those oppressions I have described, and would probably have continued in full submission had not very severe treatment in respect of tithes, united with a great speculative rise of rent about the same time, blown up the flame of resistance; the atrocious acts they were guilty of made them the object of general indignation; acts were passed for their punishment, which seemed calculated for the meridian of Barbary. This arose to such a height that by one they were to be hanged under circumstances without the common formalities of a trial, which, though repealed the following session, marks the spirit of punishment; while others remain yet the law of the land, that would if executed tend more to raise than quell an insurrection. From all which it is manifest that the gentlemen of Ireland never thought of a radical cure from overlooking the real cause of the disease, which in fact lay in themselves, and not in the wretches they doomed to the gallows. Let them change their own conduct entirely, and the poor will not long riot. Treat them like men who ought to be as free as yourselves. Put an end to that system of religious persecution which for seventy years has divided the kingdom against itself; in these two circumstances lies the cure of insurrection; perform them completely, and you will have an affectionate poor, instead of oppressed and discontented vassals.

A better treatment of the poor in Ireland is a very material point of the welfare of the whole British Empire. Events may happen which may convince us fatally of this truth; if not, oppression must have broken all the spirit and resentment of men. By what policy the Government of England can for so many years have permitted such an absurd system to be matured in Ireland is beyond the power of plain sense to discover.

Emigrations.

Before the American war broke out, the Irish and Scotch emigrations were a constant subject of conversation in England, and occasioned much discourse even in parliament. The common observation was, that if they were not stopped, those countries would be ruined, and they were generally attributed to a great rise of rents. Upon going over to Ireland I determined to omit no opportunities of discovering the cause and extent of this emigration, and my information, as may be seen in the minutes of the journey, was very regular. I have only a few general remarks to make on it here.

The spirit of emigration in Ireland appeared to be confined to two circumstances, the Presbyterian religion, and the linen manufacture. I heard of very few emigrants except among manufacturers of that persuasion. The Catholics never went; they seem not only tied to the country, but almost to the parish in which their ancestors lived. As to the emigration in the north it was an error in England to suppose it a novelty which arose with the increase in rents. The contrary was the fact; it had subsisted perhaps forty years, insomuch that at the ports of Belfast, Derry, etc., the passenger trade, as they called it, had long been a regular branch of commerce, which employed several ships, and consisted in carrying people to America. The increasing population of the country made it an increasing trade, but when the linen trade was low, the passenger trade was always high. At the time of Lord Donegan letting his estate in the north, the linen business suffered a temporary decline, which sent great numbers to America, and gave rise to the error that it was occasioned by the increase of his rents. The fact, however, was otherwise, for great numbers of those who went from his lands actually sold those leases for considerable sums, the hardship of which was supposed to have driven them to America. Some emigration, therefore, always existed, and its increase depended on the fluctuations of linen; but as to the effect there was as much error in the conclusions drawn in England as before in the cause.

It is the misfortune of all manufactures worked for a foreign market to be upon an insecure footing; periods of declension will come, and when in consequence of them great numbers of people are out of employment, the best circumstance is their enlisting in the army or navy, and it is the common result; but unfortunately the manufacture in Ireland (of which I shall have occasion to speak more hereafter) is not confined as it ought to be to towns, but spreads into all cabins of the country. Being half farmers, half manufacturers, they have too much property in cattle, etc., to enlist when idle; if they convert it into cash it will enable them to pay their passage to America, an alternative always chosen in preference to the military life. The consequence is, that they must live without work till their substance is quite consumed before they will enlist. Men who are in such a situation that from various causes they cannot work, and won't enlist, should emigrate; if they stay at home they must remain a burthen upon the community. Emigration should not, therefore, be condemned in states so ill-governed as to possess many people willing to work, but without employment.

SECTION II.—Roads, Cars.

For a country, so very far behind us as Ireland, to have got suddenly so much the start of us in the article of roads, is a spectacle that cannot fail to strike the English traveller exceedingly. But from this commendation the turnpikes in general must be excluded; they are as bad as the bye-roads are admirable. It is a common complaint that the tolls of the turnpikes are so many jobs, and the roads left in a state that disgrace the kingdom.

The following is the system on which the cross-roads are made. Any person wishing to make or mend a road has it measured by two persons, who swear to the measurement before a justice of the peace. It is described as leading from one market-town to another (it matters not in what direction), that it will be a public good, and that it will require such a sum per perch of twenty-one feet, to make or repair the same. A certificate to this purpose (of which printed forms are sold), with the blanks filled up, is signed by the measurers, and also by two persons called overseers, one of whom is usually the person applying for the road, the other the labourer he intends to employ as an overseer of the work, which overseer swears also before the justice the truth of the valuation. The certificate thus prepared is given by any person to some one of the grand jury, at either of the assizes, but usually in the spring. When all the common business of trials is over, the jury meets on that of roads; the chairman reads the certificates, and they are all put to the vote, whether to be granted or not. If rejected, they are torn in pieces and no further notice taken; if granted, they are put on the file.

This vote of approbation, without any further form, enables the person who applied for the presentment immediately to construct or repair the road in question, which he must do at his own expense; he must finish it by the following assizes, when he is to send a certificate of his having expended the money pursuant to the application; this certificate is signed by the foreman, who also signs an order on the treasurer of the county to pay him, which is done immediately. In like manner are bridges, houses of correction, gaols, etc. etc., built and repaired. If a bridge over a river which parts two counties, half is done by one and the other half by the other county.

The expense of these works is raised by a tax on the lands, paid by the tenant; in some counties it is acreable, but in others it is on the plough land, and as no two plough lands are of the same size, is a very unequal tax. In the county of Meath it is acreable, and amounts to one shilling per acre, being the highest in Ireland; but in general it is from threepence to sixpence per acre, and amounts of late years through the whole kingdom to one hundred and forty thousand pounds a year.

The juries will very rarely grant a presentment for a road which amounts to above fifty pounds, or for more than six or seven shillings a perch, so that if a person wants more to be made than such a sum will do, he divides it into two or three different measurements or presentments. By the Act of Parliament, all presentment-roads must be twenty-one feet wide at least from fence to fence, and fourteen feet of it formed with stone or gravel.

As the power of the grand jury extends in this manner to the cutting new roads where none ever were before, as well as to the repairing and widening old ones, exclusive, however, of parks, gardens, etc., it was necessary to put a restriction against the wanton expense of it. Any presentment may be traversed that is opposed, by denying the allegations of the certificate; this is sure of delaying it until another assizes, and in the meantime persons are appointed to view the line of road demanded, and report on the necessity or hardship of the case. The payment of the money may also be traversed after the certificate of its being laid out; for if any person views and finds it a manifest imposition and job, he has that power to delay payment until the cause is cleared up and proved. But this traverse is not common. Any persons are eligible for asking presentments; but it is usually done only by resident gentlemen, agents, clergy, or respectable tenantry. It follows necessarily, that every person is desirous of making the roads leading to his own house, and that private interest alone is considered in it, which I have heard objected to the measure; but this I must own appears to me the great merit of it. Whenever individuals act for the public alone, the public is very badly served; but when the pursuit of their own interest is the way to benefit the public, then is the public good sure to be promoted; such is the case of presentment of roads: for a few years the good roads were all found leading from houses like rays from a centre, with a surrounding space, without any communication; but every year brought the remedy, until in a short time, those rays pointing from so many centres met, and then the communication was complete. The original Act passed but seventeen years ago, and the effect of it in all parts of the kingdom is so great, that I found it perfectly practicable to travel upon wheels by a map; I will go here; I will go there; I could trace a route upon paper as wild as fancy could dictate, and everywhere I found beautiful roads without break or hindrance, to enable me to realise my design. What a figure would a person make in England, who should attempt to move in that manner, where the roads, as Dr. Burn has well observed, are almost in as bad a state as in the time of Philip and Mary. In a few years there will not be a piece of bad road except turnpikes in all Ireland. The money raised for this first and most important of all national purposes, is expended among the people who pay it, employs themselves and their teams, encourages their agriculture, and facilitates so greatly the improvement of waste lands, that it ought always to be considered as the first step to any undertaking of that sort.

At first, roads, in common with bridges, were paid out of the general treasure of the county, but by a subsequent act the road tax is now on baronies; each barony pays for its own roads. By another act juries were enabled to grant presentments of narrow mountain roads, at two shillings and sixpence a perch. By another, they were empowered to grant presentments of footpaths, by the side of roads, at one shilling a perch. By a very late act, they are also enabled to contract at three-halfpence per perch per annum from the first making of a road, for keeping it in repair, which before could not be done without a fresh presentment. Arthur King, Esq. of Moniva, whose agriculture is described in the preceding minutes, and who at that time represented the county of Galway, was the worthy citizen who first brought this excellent measure into parliament: Ireland, and every traveller that ever visits it ought, to the latest time, to revere the memory of such a distinguished benefactor to the public. Before that time the roads, like those of England, remained impassable, under the miserable police of the six days' labour. Similar good effects would here flow from adopting the measure, which would ease the kingdom of a great burthen in its public effects absolutely contemptible; and the tax here, as in Ireland, ought to be so laid, as to be borne by the tenant whose business it is at present to repair.

Upon the imperfections of the Irish system I have only to remark, that juries should, in some cases, be more ready than they are to grant these presentments. In general, they are extremely liberal, but sometimes they take silly freaks of giving none, or very few. Experience having proved, from the general goodness of the roads, that abuses cannot be very great, they should go on with spirit to perfect the great work throughout the kingdom; and as a check upon those who lay out the money, it might perhaps be advisable to print county maps of the presentment roads, with corresponding lists and tables of the names of all persons who have obtained presentments, the sums they received, and for what roads. These should be given freely by the jurymen, to all their acquaintance, that every man might know, to whose carelessness or jobbing the public was indebted for bad roads, when they had paid for good ones. Such a practice would certainly deter many.

At 11,042,642 acres in the kingdom, £140,000 a year amounts to just threepence an acre for the whole territory: a very trifling tax for such an improvement, and which almost ranks in public ease and benefit with that of the post-office.

SECTION III.—Manners and Customs.

It is but an illiberal business for a traveller, who designs to publish remarks upon a country to sit down coolly in his closet and write a satire on the inhabitants. Severity of that sort must be enlivened with an uncommon share of wit and ridicule, to please. Where very gross absurdities are found, it is fair and manly to note them; but to enter into character and disposition is generally uncandid, since there are no people but might be better than they are found, and none but have virtues which deserve attention, at least as much as their failings; for these reasons this section would not have found a place in my observations, had not some persons, of much more flippancy than wisdom, given very gross misrepresentations of the Irish nation. It is with pleasure, therefore, that I take up the pen on the present occasion; as a much longer residence there enables me to exhibit a very different picture; in doing this, I shall be free to remark, wherein I think the conduct of certain classes may have given rise to general and consequently injurious condemnation.

There are three races of people in Ireland, so distinct as to strike the least attentive traveller: these are the Spanish which are found in Kerry, and a part of Limerick and Cork, tall and thin, but well made, a long visage, dark eyes, and long black lank hair. The time is not remote when the Spaniards had a kind of settlement on the coast of Kerry, which seemed to be overlooked by government. There were many of them in Queen Elizabeth's reign, nor were they entirely driven out till the time of Cromwell. There is an island of Valentia on that coast, with various other names, certainly Spanish. The Scotch race is in the north, where are to be found the feature which are supposed to mark that people, their accent and many of their customs. In a district near Dublin, but more particularly in the baronies of Bargie and Forth in the county of Wexford, the Saxon tongue is spoken without any mixture of the Irish, and the people have a variety of customs mentioned in the minutes, which distinguish them from their neighbours. The rest of the kingdom is made up of mongrels. The Milesian race of Irish, which may be called native, are scattered over the kingdom, but chiefly found in Connaught and Munster; a few considerable families, whose genealogy is undoubted, remain, but none of them with considerable possessions except the O'Briens and Mr. O'Neil; the former have near twenty thousand pounds a year in the family, the latter half as much, the remnant of a property once his ancestors, which now forms six or seven of the greatest estates in the kingdom. O'Hara and M'Dermot are great names in Connaught, and O'Donnohue a considerable one in Kerry; but I heard of a family of O'Drischal's in Cork, who claim an origin prior in Ireland to any of the Milesian race.

The only divisions which a traveller, who passed through the kingdom without making any residence could make, would be into people of considerable fortune and mob. The intermediate division of the scale, so numerous and respectable in England, would hardly attract the least notice in Ireland. A residence in the kingdom convinces one, however, that there is another class in general of small fortune—country gentlemen and renters of land. The manners, habits, and customs of people of considerable fortune are much the same everywhere, at least there is very little difference between England and Ireland, it is among the common people one must look for those traits by which we discriminate a national character. The circumstances which struck me most in the common Irish were, vivacity and a great and eloquent volubility of speech; one would think they could take snuff and talk without tiring till doomsday. They are infinitely more cheerful and lively than anything we commonly see in England, having nothing of that incivility of sullen silence with which so many Englishmen seem to wrap themselves up, as if retiring within their own importance. Lazy to an excess at work, but so spiritedly active at play, that at hurling, which is the cricket of savages, they shew the greatest feats of agility. Their love of society is as remarkable as their curiosity is insatiable; and their hospitality to all comers, be their own poverty ever so pinching, has too much merit to be forgotten. Pleased to enjoyment with a joke, or witty repartee, they will repeat it with such expression, that the laugh will be universal. Warm friends and revengeful enemies; they are inviolable in their secrecy, and inevitable in their resentment; with such a notion of honour, that neither threat nor reward would induce them to betray the secret or person of a man, though an oppressor, whose property they would plunder without ceremony. Hard drinkers and quarrelsome; great liars, but civil, submissive, and obedient. Dancing is so universal among them, that there are everywhere itinerant dancing-masters, to whom the cottars pay sixpence a quarter for teaching their families. Besides the Irish jig, which they can dance with a most luxuriant expression, minuets and country-dances are taught; and I even heard some talk of cotillions coming in.

Some degree of education is also general, hedge schools, as they are called, (they might as well be termed ditch ones, for I have seen many a ditch full of scholars,) are everywhere to be met with where reading and writing are taught; schools are also common for men; I have seen a dozen great fellows at school, and was told they were educating with an intention of being priests. Many strokes in their character are evidently to be ascribed to the extreme oppression under which they live. If they are as great thieves and liars as they are reported, it is certainly owing to this cause.

If from the lowest class we rise to the highest, all there is gaiety, pleasure, luxury, and extravagance; the town life at Dublin is formed on the model of that of London. Every night in the winter there is a ball or a party, where the polite circle meet, not to enjoy but to sweat each other; a great crowd crammed into twenty feet square gives a zest to the agréments of small talk and whist. There are four or five houses large enough to receive a company commodiously, but the rest are so small as to make parties detestable. There is however an agreeable society in Dublin, in which a man of large fortune will not find his time heavy. The style of living may be guessed from the fortunes of the resident nobility and great commoners; there are about thirty that possess incomes from seven to twenty thousand pounds a year. The court has nothing remarkable or splendid in it, but varies very much, according to the private fortune or liberality of disposition in the lord lieutenant.

In the country their life has some circumstances which are not commonly seen in England. Large tracts of land are kept in hand by everybody to supply the deficiencies of markets; this gives such a plenty, that, united with the lowness of taxes and prices, one would suppose it difficult for them to spend their incomes, if Dublin in the winter did not lend assistance. Let it be considered that the prices of meat are much lower than in England; poultry only a fourth of the price; wild fowl and fish in vastly greater plenty; rum and brandy not half the price; coffee, tea, and wines far cheaper; labour not above a third; servants' wages upon an average thirty per cent. cheaper. That taxes are inconsiderable, for there is no land-tax, no poor-rates, no window tax, no candle or soap tax, only half a wheel-tax, no servants' tax, and a variety of other articles heavily burdened in England, but not in Ireland. Considering all this, one would think they could not spend their incomes; they do contrive it, however. In this business they are assisted by two customs that have an admirable tendency to it, great numbers of horses and servants.

In England such extensive demesnes would be parks around the seats for beauty as much as use, but it is not so in Ireland; the words deer-park and demesne are to be distinguished; there are great demesnes without any parks, but a want of taste, too common in Ireland, is having a deer-park at a distance from the house; the residence surrounded by walls, or hedges, or cabins; and the lawn inclosure scattered with animals of various sorts, perhaps three miles off. The small quantity of corn proportioned to the total acres, shows how little tillage is attended to even by those who are the best able to carry it on; and the column of turnips proves in the clearest manner what the progress of improvement is in that kingdom. The number of horses may almost be esteemed a satire upon common sense; were they well fed enough to be useful, they would not be so numerous, but I have found a good hack for a common ride scarce in a house where there were a hundred. Upon an average, the horses in gentlemen's stables throughout the kingdom are not fed half so well as they are in England by men of equal fortune; yet the number makes the expense of them very heavy.

Another circumstance to be remarked in the country life is the miserableness of many of their houses; there are men of five thousand a year in Ireland, who live in habitations that a man of seven hundred a year in England would disdain; an air of neatness, order, dress, and propreté, is wanting to a surprising degree around the mansion; even new and excellent houses have often nothing of this about them. But the badness of the houses is remedying every hour throughout the whole kingdom, for the number of new ones just built, or building, is prodigiously great. I should suppose there were not ten dwellings in the kingdom thirty years ago that were fit for an English pig to live in. Gardens were equally bad, but now they are running into the contrary extreme, and wall in five, six, ten, and even twenty Irish acres for a garden, but generally double or treble what is necessary.

The tables of people of fortune are very plentifully spread; many elegantly, differing in nothing from those of England. I think I remarked that venison wants the flavour it has with us, probably for the same reason, that the produce of rich parks is never equal to that of poor ones; the moisture of the climate, and the richness of the soil, give fat but not flavour. Another reason is the smallness of the parks, a man who has three or four thousand acres in his hands, has not perhaps above three or four hundred in his deer-park, and range is a great point for good venison. Nor do I think that garden vegetables have the flavour found in those of England, certainly owing to the climate; green peas I found everywhere perfectly insipid, and lettuce, etc., not good. Claret is the common wine of all tables, and so much inferior to what is drunk in

England, that it does not appear to be the same wine; but their port is incomparable, so much better than the English, as to prove, if proof was wanting, the abominable adulterations it must undergo with us. Drinking and duelling are two charges which have long been alleged against the gentlemen of Ireland, but the change of manners which has taken place in that kingdom is not generally known in England. Drunkenness ought no longer to be a reproach, for at every table I was at in Ireland I saw a perfect freedom reign, every person drank just as little as they pleased, nor have I ever been asked to drink a single glass more than I had an inclination for; I may go farther and assert that hard drinking is very rare among people of fortune; yet it is certain that they sit much longer at table than in England. I was much surprised at first going over to find no summons to coffee, the company often sitting till eight, nine, or ten o'clock before they went to the ladies. If a gentleman likes tea or coffee, he retires without saying anything; a stranger of rank may propose it to the master of the house, who from custom contrary to that of England, will not stir till he receives such a hint, as they think it would imply a desire to save their wine. If the gentlemen were generally desirous of tea, I take it for granted they would have it, but their slighting is one inconvenience to such as desire it, not knowing when it is provided, conversation may carry them beyond the time, and then if they do trifle over the coffee it will certainly be cold. There is a want of attention in this, which the ladies should remedy, if they will not break the old custom and send to the gentlemen, which is what they ought to do, they certainly should have a salver fresh. I must, however, remark, that at the politest tables, which are those of people who have resided much out of Ireland, this point is conducted exactly as it is in England.

Duelling was once carried to an excess, which was a real reproach and scandal to the kingdom; it of course proceeded from excessive drinking; as the cause has disappeared, the effect has nearly followed; not however, entirely, for it is yet far more common among people of fashion than in England. Of all practices, a man who felt for the honour of his country would wish soonest to banish this, for there is not one favourable conclusion to be drawn from it: as to courage, nobody can question that of a polite and enlightened nation, entitled to a share of the reputation of the age; but it implies uncivilised manners, an ignorance of those forms which govern polite societies, or else a brutal drunkenness; the latter is no longer the cause or the pretence. As to the former, they would place the national character so backward, would take from it so much of its pretence to civilisation, elegance and politeness of manners, that no true Irishman would be pleased with the imputation. Certain it is, that none are so captious as those who think themselves neglected or despised; and none are so ready to believe themselves either one or the other as persons unused to good company. Captious people, therefore, who are ready to take an affront, must inevitably have been accustomed to ill company, unless there should be something uncommonly crooked in their natural dispositions, which is not to be supposed. Let every man that fights his one, two, three, or half-a-dozen duels, receive it as a maxim, that every one he adds to the number is but an additional proof of his being ill-educated, and having vitiated his manners by the contagion of bad company; who is it that can reckon the most numerous rencontres? who but the bucks, bloods, landjobbers, and little drunken country gentlemen? Ought not people of fashion to blush at a practice which will very soon be the distinction only of the most contemptible of the people? the point of honour will and must remain for the decision of certain affronts, but it will rarely be had recourse to in polite, sensible, and well-bred company. The practice among real gentlemen in Ireland every day declining is a strong proof that a knowledge of the world corrects the old manners, and consequently its having ever been prevalent was owing to the causes to which I have attributed it.

There is another point of manners somewhat connected with the present subject, which partly induced me to place a motto at the head of this section. It is the conduct of juries; the criminal law of Ireland is the same as that of England, but in the execution it is so different as scarcely to be known. I believe it is a fact, at least I have been assured so, that no man was ever hanged in Ireland for killing another in a duel: the security is such that nobody ever thought of removing out of the way of justice, yet there have been deaths of that sort, which had no more to do with honour than stabbing in the dark. I believe Ireland is the only country in Europe, I am sure it is the only part of the British dominions, where associations among men of fortune are necessary for apprehending ravishers. It is scarcely credible how many young women have even of late years been ravished, and carried off in order (as they generally have fortunes) to gain to appearance a voluntary marriage. These actions, it is true, are not committed by the class I am considering at present; but they are tried by them, and acquitted. I think there has been only one man executed for that crime, which is so common as to occasion the associations I mentioned; it is to this supine execution of the law that such enormities are owing. Another circumstance which has the effect of screening all sorts of offenders, is men of fortune protecting them, and making interest for their acquittal, which is attended with a variety of evil consequences. I heard it boasted in the county of Fermanagh, that there had not been a man hanged in it for two-and-twenty years; all I concluded from this was, that there had been many a jury who deserved it richly.

Let me, however, conclude what I have to observe on the conduct of the principal people residing in Ireland, that there are great numbers among them who are as liberal in all their ideas as any people in Europe; that they have seen the errors which have given an ill character to the manners of their country, and done everything that example could effect to produce a change: that that happy change has been partly effected, and is effecting every hour, insomuch that a man may go into a vast variety of families which he will find actuated by no other principles than those of the most cultivated politeness, and the most liberal urbanity.

But I must now come to another class of people, to whose conduct it is almost entirely owing that the character of the nation has not that lustre abroad, which I dare assert it will soon very generally merit: this is the class of little country gentlemen; tenants, who drink their claret by means of profit rents; jobbers in farms; bucks; your fellows with round hats, edged with gold, who hunt in the day, get drunk in the evening, and fight the next morning. I shall not dwell on a subject so perfectly disagreeable, but remark that these are the men among whom drinking, wrangling, quarrelling, fighting, ravishing, etc. etc. are found as in their native soil; once to a degree that made them a pest of society; they are growing better, but even now, one or two of them got by accident (where they have no business) into better company are sufficient very much to derange the pleasures that result from a liberal conversation. A new spirit; new fashions; new modes of politeness exhibited by the higher ranks are imitated by the lower, which will, it is to be hoped, put an end to this race of beings; and either drive their sons and cousins into the army or navy, or sink them into plain farmers like those we have in England, where it is common to see men with much greater property without pretending to be gentlemen. I repeat it from the intelligence I received, that even this class are very different from what they were twenty years ago, and improve so fast that the time will soon come when the national character will not be degraded by any set.

That character is upon the whole respectable: it would be unfair to attribute to the nation at large the vices and follies of only one class of individuals. Those persons from whom it is candid to take a general estimate do credit to their country. That they are a people learned, lively, and ingenious, the admirable authors they have produced will be an eternal monument; witness their Swift, Sterne, Congreve, Boyle, Berkeley, Steele, Farquhar, Southerne, and Goldsmith. Their talent for eloquence is felt, and acknowledged in the parliaments of both the kingdoms. Our own service both by sea and land, as well as that (unfortunately for us) of the principal monarchies of Europe, speak their steady and determined courage. Every unprejudiced traveller who visits them will be as much pleased with their cheerfulness, as obliged by their hospitality; and will find them a brave, polite, and liberal people.

18617116R00047

Printed in Great Britain
by Amazon